"Phil Allen reveals the pain of racial wounds and the power of the healing God. Allen takes you on a painful journey into healing and wholeness. Allen echoes the lingering pain of hidden hurts and the revelation of the power of the God who heals."

—Kenneth C. Ulmer, DMin, PhD, presiding bishop, The King's University, Macedonia International Bible Fellowship

"Phil Allen is among the most gifted leaders I have had the privilege to meet. Everything he does is exceptional, from being an athlete, a model, a poet, a preacher, and now an author. Nothing remains the same after Phil touches it. It is only fitting that *Open Wounds* and the issue of racial injustice is addressed by this prolific personality. Who better to reach back from his many accomplishments to festering issues others have overlooked or deliberately ignored and bring redemptive solutions?"

—Larry Titus, president, Kingdom Global Ministries; author of *The Teleios Man*

"Phil Allen's story is as unique as any personal, multigenerational African American tragedy can be. And that means the narrative is also a painfully common one. *Open Wounds* names the reality: for himself, for his family, for this nation. What makes Allen's story so powerful is his pursuit of the facts, the implications, and the risks of healing. But in the end, it is less a hero's journey and more a communal story of lived faith, honest communion, and dogged hope."

—Mark Labberton, president, Fuller Theological Seminary

"It is only in the most technical sense of the word that Phil Allen Jr. was once a doctoral student of mine. In actual fact, in numerous ways that extend far beyond the classroom, I am his student. It is an honor to learn from him. Full stop. But in times like this, his wisdom has never been more necessary and urgent, for it quite literally concerns the difference between life and death. I can't force you to sit at Phil's feet as he teaches us, but I invite you to do so. Speaking from personal experience, I promise you that if you do, you will never be the same."

—Kutter Callaway, PhD, associate professor, theology and culture, Fuller Theological Seminary; codirector of *Reel Spirituality*; and author of *The Aesthetics of Atheism*

"*Open Wounds* is a masterfully written gem! Phil writes on a topic that too many of us carry: *pain*. He captures something that many of us have developed: *resilience*. He illuminates what we all need: *healing*. It's a must read!"

—Johnny C. Shelton, chaplain, spiritual advisor, and life coach, Baltimore Ravens; president/founder of Attitudes in Motion Inc.

"Phil Allen weaves a powerful truth of sin, violence, tragedy, and pain, which were wrong every which way you see them but prevalent and largely justified by white Americans more than sixty years ago. The ongoing struggles to cope with anger, passing that anger from generation to generation, leave a permanent mark of traumatic distress.

"Regrettably, similar actions with the same tragic results are on the rise again in 2020.

"The impact of pain from a violent death in the family runs deep and wide, like water pulsating from the intersection of the river into the open sea. It's a legacy of pain seeping through the void left from the unspoken secrets of the *Open Wounds*."

—Reena Evers-Everette, executive director, Medgar and Myrlie Evers Institute

"Phil Allen Jr., in *Open Wounds*, takes us inside the trauma center of African American racial pain. He uses the intergenerational lens of his father's traumatic loss to explain Black rage as the abused offspring of white supremacy. This is a must read for all interested in the racial healing of the United States of America!"

—Jerry Taylor, associate professor of the Bible,
Abilene Christian University

"Phil Allen has written a haunting and painfully honest book. *Open Wounds* is the story of yet another Black family forced to deal with the tragedy of racial terror and the trauma it inflicts on the entire family over generations. Fortunately, the story does not end with racial trauma; it unveils the journey toward racial healing and offers a way for others to experience the process of racial wholeness."

—John Williams, director, Center for
Racial Reconciliation

"*Open Wounds* uniquely divulges the destructive power and tragic reality of racial violence that intergenerationally affects African American families. Through powerful personal narratives running three generations, Phil Allen convincingly demonstrates that racial violence not just damages the victim but harms surrounding family members and future generations. He is successful in not only pinpointing the undeniable impact of racial trauma but also offering a rich and thoughtful theological reflection of the topic. A powerful living testimony against a postracial ideology, I strongly recommend this book for those interested in the study of the interconnected psychological, cultural, and theological dimensions of racism."

—Hak Joon Lee, Lewis B. Smedes
Professor of Christian Ethics,
Fuller Theological Seminary

"Phil Allen tells a profoundly moving story of the generational impact of a family trauma. White Christians who are seeking to understand the response of anger to incidents that lead to the deaths of Black men and women should listen carefully to this narrative. Allen's explanation of the events helps us understand his particular experience and better understand the pain expressed by people of color in other circumstances. Allen leaves us with a redemptive vision, pointing to practices that form us as people of faith in solidarity with our brothers and sisters of color. I will be using this book in my classes to help foster reflection on how to grow into a faith community that embodies a biblical call to equity and inclusion."

—Susan L. Maros, MDiv, PhD, affiliate assistant professor, Christian leadership, Fuller Theological Seminary

"Phil Allen Jr. has written a must-read personal narrative for anyone grappling with intergenerational trauma. *Open Wounds* highlights unresolved and cyclical pain associated with racism in the American South while offering tools for embarking on a journey toward healing."

—Tanya E. Walker-Bethea, PhD, associate professor, African American literature, Winston-Salem State University

"Phil Allen's masterful use of prose, story, and theological frameworks allows the reader to experience a narrative that is all too intimate for some and absolutely remote for others. While many are dealing with racism and systemic evils in theoretical arenas, Allen crafts an invitation to the living room of concretized and experienced ramifications in order to arrive at approaches to healing that represent an embodied theology."

—Dwight Radcliff, PhD, assistant professor of mission, theology, and culture, Fuller Theological Seminary; academic dean, Pannell Center for Black Church Studies

Open Wounds

Open Wounds

*A Story of Racial Tragedy,
Trauma, and Redemption*

Phil Allen Jr.

FORTRESS PRESS
MINNEAPOLIS

OPEN WOUNDS
A Story of Racial Tragedy, Trauma, and Redemption

Cover image: From the personal collection of Phil Allen Jr.
Cover design: Alisha Lofgren

Print ISBN: 978-1-5064-6933-1
eBook ISBN: 978-1-5064-6934-8

To my grandfather
Nate Allen
and my grandmother
Rebecca Allen Young,

I hope to make you proud.

To my father,
Phillip Allen Sr.; Nate Allen;
Naomi Allen; and Eric Allen (RIP),

your father's life mattered.

To my siblings,
Sherrie, Kelle, Olivia, and Nicholas,
and

to my cousins
Jonathan, Mechelle, Dante, and Trevor,

may this story remind you
of not just our family's pain but also our resiliency.

To the next generation,
Kearsin, Elizabeth, and Nicholas,

know your history and
never be afraid to tell your stories.

Contents

Acknowledgments

There is a host of family and friends I could list that contributed to the whole *Open Wounds* project. For the sake of space, I want to acknowledge key people who were integral to the publishing of this book.

We all need someone who believes in us and in the work that we do. Kutter Callaway has been alongside me for the past few years encouraging me with this project. Thank you for believing in this story and being an advocating voice for *Open Wounds*.

No matter what we pursue in life, we all need mentors, coaches, and experts whose voices and insights make the project better. Thank you, Dr. Tracy Swinton Bailey and Dr. Tanya Walker-Bethea, for your coaching that helped make me a better writer. We go back to elementary and middle school, respectively. Who would have thought when we were in the tenth grade taking honors English together that we would be working on a book together over thirty years later?

I want to say thank you to my mom, Vernelle Sherald Brown, for always being my cheerleader behind the scenes supporting me. Every piece of poetry in this book was first inspired by your poetry when I was a kid.

To two young ladies who were the first to have a set of eyes editing and proofreading for me, you set the tone. Thank you, Rachel Paprocki and Kareena Kirlew.

To all of you (and you know who you are, too many to name) who supported the film and this book in prayer and in financial support, I see you and thank you.

PART I

Telling Tragedy

Introduction

Telling a Tragedy

Racism is a thief and a murderer
A deserter
Of all that is good
It preys on bodies of color
Even while a body of color prays
The darker the skin
The more destructive is the pursuit of this kind
Of sin

F or most of my life, he was a ghost, a mythical fig-
ure, maybe even a figment of my family's collective
imagination. There were no pictures of him around
the house or hidden away in some dust-covered trunk
serving as a treasure chest of ancestral memorabilia. There
was never any conversation about him over the course
of my life until I reached the age of forty-two. I was left
to take the morsels of comments about him sporadically
shared throughout the years and piece together the biogra-
phy of my grandfather. To relieve the secret anxiety and curiosity I had as I grew older, I attempted to convince myself
that he never existed in the first place. However, this was
in vain.

All my life I created an image of my grandfather; this image was not based on who I knew him to be or what I heard about him but instead based on who I hoped he would have been in my life had he been alive. I would wonder how different or the same the grandfather I never knew would have been compared with the only living grandfather who played a role in my upbringing. I wondered how much of my father was like him. I wouldn't say it was painful at the time, but I knew there was a void in my family. I knew I yearned for answers. I have come to learn that my father had to do the same thing, imagine who his father would have been to him. It became clear to me that he also felt the same as I did—he wanted to have answers to fill the void. He and I both needed a figurative gauze to cover the open wound so that healing might begin.

A Tragic Story

What should have been a day of worship and gratitude for God's blessings and mercy turned out to be a day of mourning. On Sunday, January 29, 1933—undoubtedly a cold southern day—my maternal great-grandfather, Bruce Harper, was killed in Alabama while traveling in search of work during the height of the Great Depression. Always vulnerable to the racial climate, he was pushed off a train to a violent death. Uncertain if he was traveling to or from Alabama back to South Carolina, what was certain is that he would never see his baby girl grow up. My grandmother was just two years old in 1933, when her father was killed. She had no memory of him. White supremacy not only snuffed out the full-grown body of her father but also caused an abortion of nascent memories of father-daughter moments before they could fully develop in her mind.

This was not the only time a man in my family was killed "at the hands of racism." Barely a generation later in 1953, Nathaniel "Nate" Allen, my paternal grandfather, was murdered in the Sampit River of Georgetown, South Carolina. His body was found after a few days submerged underwater, lying facedown in the river with a bullet hole in the back of his head, or in his back, depending on which version of the story one hears. An apparent altercation between him and three white men led to my grandfather's attempt to escape a gun pointed directly at him. He never made it to the refuge of the river that he hoped would save his life.

Two fathers were taken from their homes and families because the color of their skin rendered them vulnerable in a culture that perpetuated racially motivated injustices. In 1930s and 1950s America, racism was able to flourish because Black men's ancestral heritage was despised by white racists in a nation with a history of trauma from bigotry, systemic inequities, and a cultural ethos. However, these events are not just about what happened to a single family over sixty years ago. This is a story that reflects what was indicative of the times my grandfather and great-grandfather lived in. It is about the legacy that such practices have left for us to navigate and attempt to heal from even today. This is about the need to connect the dots between the blatancy of our racist past and both the obvious and the insidious subtleties of our racist present—to show how trauma has transgenerational and intergenerational effects, particularly on African American families and particularly on African American sons like me.

Truth Born Again

I was in my late thirties when I summoned the courage to initiate a much-needed conversation with my paternal grandmother, Rebecca Allen Young. I asked her about the details surrounding my grandfather's death. She was visibly upset by the idea of a conversation reliving arguably the most painful time in her life. I could see the tightness in her face and the clutching of her hands as she tried to avoid the question. In that moment, I recognized the lasting trauma that persisted not only in my grandmother but most likely as an undercurrent for my whole family. For my grandmother, it did not matter that I wanted to learn more about who my grandfather may or may not have been. Her emotional response to my genuine curiosity to know about our family history and the events surrounding my grandfather's passing was telling of the horror I was asking her to relive. It was not until less than a year from her passing that I revisited the question, hoping for her to have a conversation rather than shutting it down.

It comes as no surprise to me that my father never spoke about his father to me or my siblings our entire lives until just a couple of years before the writing of this book. I have long believed the absence of his father and the reason for his absence in our lives was the root of his choosing to medicate in self-destructive ways for decades. Open wounds require attention. Neither silence nor amnesia is a healthy or sufficient way to respond to physical, emotional, or mental violation—no matter how far in the past they may have occurred.

For all these reasons and more, my hopes for this book and any corresponding projects on this matter are the following: (1) that healing for my family can begin in some ways and deepen in others, (2) that the countless African American families with similar stories as far back as the Jim Crow lynching era and as recent as the families of Trayvon Martin or Ahmaud Arbery may be inspired to tell their stories as well, and (3) that this story becomes a catalyst for understanding the larger narrative of intergenerational trauma from racism, leading to concrete progress toward racial *solidarity* in America.

In response to the discourse of racism (the system) that is grounded in white supremacy (the undergirding ideology or spirit) and manifested in tragic ways, such as slavery and Jim Crow, white people tend to insist on forgetting about the past and just moving on. This is a dangerous proposition. Some people do not realize that we are living out the legacy of our past every day. The events of 150 years ago—at the tail end of slavery—still have effects in our present. The physical and psychological residues of white supremacy are present in the self-perception of both white and Black people as well as these groups' perceptions of each other. The tension is present and further thickens with every act of bigotry or perceived racism across this nation. Events today do not stand alone. They are but pieces of a historical puzzle of events that form a picture of the cultural ethos of the United States. Each and every one of these events, like those of the past, is a traumatic experience that does not just go away when we close our eyes and plug our ears. As a case in point, to this day, my father and his siblings have carried the trauma of losing a father to a racist act that culminated in the injustice of a lie written and authenticated on his death certificate.

Intergenerational trauma is the overarching theme that hovers over the tragic events surrounding my grandfather's murder. I received what my father carried and passed on to my siblings and me whether consciously or not. He received the trauma of an absent father due to racial injustice. I inherited the pain of my father and grandmother. Without healing in our family, the next generation will inherit the same. They will take the baton of bitterness and continue a never-ending sprint to the finish line of toxicity, despair, and a false sense of wholeness. They will literally carry the trauma in their bodies. As such, I hope to uncover not only how events of the past have shaped individuals and groups but also how events, laws, policies, and narratives have deformed our physiological and cultural DNA. Central to this malformed social genetic code is the imposition of "whiteness." I want to examine the ideology and principality of whiteness. This is not so much a discussion of white persons of particular ethnic groups with white skin—although white people are the primary agents of whiteness—but a way of thinking and being in the world, especially from a position of or in association with power.

The end goal for this book and corresponding projects is redemption. A friend of mine mentioned to me on social media that she was curious to see how redemption would look. My grandfather's name and life are deserving of redemption. My grandfather's service in the US Navy is deserving of recognition. The details of the events surrounding his murder—which will likely never be resolved due to time and the deaths of many of those involved sixty-seven years ago—deserve to be heard. Redemption is in the healing of a son who lost his father at two years old and has medicated with violence, drugs, and alcohol for most of his life. Redemption is Nate Allen's name intertwined in his grandson's quest to facilitate racial justice and solidarity. The hope is that his death was not in vain. Instead, it will become a catalytic episode within the narrative of justice and the work of solidarity, though delayed by several decades.

Ultimately, although unlikely, redemption is the reopening of my grandfather's cold case to publicly declare the correct cause of his death. Redemption is inspiring more stories that lie dormant on the basement floors of the hearts and minds of families who have experienced such injustice without anyone being held accountable. Redemption is when the nation is forced to look more deeply into its past and understand its links to the present and future, leading to genuine collective repentance. Redemption is restorative justice for African American families who have had property, opportunities, and persons taken away from them while permitted by the complicity of US institutions and agencies. Redemption is racial solidarity from the shared lament and practices that transcend race and seek to eradicate the residue of a racist past that continues to exert its influence on us today.

When Calling Calls

I recently spoke with a fellow seminarian and classmate, Inés Velasquez-McBryde, who was in attendance when I first shared these thoughts about my grandfather's death in a class we took together. She not only confirmed what I thought people felt about it but also shared even more profound thoughts about that moment. She said,

> It was your lived faith . . . the historicity of race in your family . . . an embodied theology . . . a calling and conviction of healing and reconciliation. More than anything I was also moved that you're called to heal

wounds and out of your healing a tidal wave of healing to others. It's lived witness. It's testimony. The story itself hits our wombs and hearts as it does, as you tell it. Your story brought us near you because it moved us towards love and solidarity. That's what storytelling does. An untold story never heals. That was catalytic storytelling that day in class in the presence of many witnesses.

In addition to Inés's comments, what deeply moved me was the authentically visceral response by my white classmates to the tragedy of racial injustice that happened to my family over sixty years ago. The moment was mutually enlightening. They caught a glimpse of the country's history in real time that made it palpable for them. They could now touch it. Yet it was just as illuminating for me to see the lament from my white brothers and sisters as well as those of other racial backgrounds in the class. It taught me that there are some who are receptive even if they do not fully understand the depth of pain of such an event and history. They played a critical role in this newly amplified voice of mine.

There was a "calling out" that unfolded in that moment, a beckoning from God giving me permission to speak these painful truths about history and its legacy even beyond my own family's narrative. This was an opportunity to become a conduit for healing wounds—my own, my father's, my peoples', and even white folks', who assume that they have been immune to the trauma of racism and that their social DNA remains unaffected by its influence. I've learned that this is what God does, calls one out to a new season of uncertain terrain through events and interactions as we live out our faith. There isn't always an audible-like "word" from the Lord that floors a person and confirms that it is indeed a divine calling. There are times when the moment, as it unfolds, is the summoning to a necessary new life trajectory—one with personal, spiritual, and social implications.

I cannot unhear this summon. All I can do is respond by inviting you to bear witness to the various open wounds that my body still bears and, in doing so, move toward healing. Healing requires "all hands on deck." It will take more than just well wishes and apologies. It takes solidarity. This calling I speak of mandates a communal effort that transcends racial lines. It is rejoicing together, grieving together, and fighting together. The balm to close and heal these wounds is found in a community where we stand in solidarity, resisting oppressive ideologies, attitudes, actions, and structures that cause the wounds in the first place.

The title of this book has multiple meanings attached to it. *Open Wounds* is in regard to the nostalgic, the tragic, and the catalytic events that have left unattended scars. After my grandfather was killed, my grandmother was never the same. It was a traumatic event that required the rest of her life and ultimately death before she was ever free from the pain of her wounds. Once my father—at nine years old—found out how his father was killed, he became a person riddled with rage and hatred. He sought self-destructive painkillers in the form of drugs, violence, and women to numb the pain from this loss. Ever since my grandmother gave me the gift of conversation centered on my grandfather's death, it sparked more than a curiosity to learn more; it fueled a fire in me to allow this tragic family history to be a catalyst for a greater narrative and cause with healing potential. I borrow from Martin Luther King Jr.'s idea that suffering can be redemptive and trauma can be fuel for moral agency—*Open Wounds* is about more than tragedy. It is about resiliency.

CHAPTER I

Before Emmett Till

Nate Allen

Strange fruit doesn't always hang from poplar trees
Sometimes they fall from branches and limbs
And they lie forgotten on the ground
Left to spoil and waste away
They are shot down
And left to float in rivers
Until the rivers vomit them to the shores and docks like
A generation of Jonahs expelled from the belly of a fish
Called whiteness
They are left to rot
In the dark of the night
In the silence of blind eyes
In the deafness of closed ears
Their lifeless eyes stare
At the earth as the dirt from which they are formed
    beckons them

This particular day in class we were watching a segment of the miniseries *Eyes on the Prize* about the civil rights movement and the events that inspired it. There was a picture on the screen of Emmett Till lying in his casket. His face, disfigured and unrecognizable, was displayed so that the world could see what anti-Black racism from white supremacy had done to a fourteen-year-old African American kid. Till was a teenager from Chicago who was visiting family in Money, Mississippi, over the summer of 1954. Apparently, Till had whistled at or said "Hey baby!" to a white woman. During that time, it was forbidden for a Black man or boy to address a white woman in any way other than submissively and respectfully—other ways would have been cause for death. Till was killed by the woman's husband and brother, who were acquitted of the murder. They later admitted in an interview, protected by the law of double jeopardy, that they had indeed killed him.[1]

Watching this film about Till's death, I was composed on the outside, but I grieved internally. I wasn't sure why revisiting a picture I had been familiar with since I was Till's age had stirred me up as much as it had. But rather than seeing Till, I saw my grandfather.

I had no idea these emotions about my grandfather's death were just beneath the surface of my conscience. All it would take was an image in a documentary to bring them to the surface. My stomach would begin to feel unsettled. My eyes would dampen with tears too stubborn to remain hidden. My emotions danced back and forth between anger and sadness. Little did I know that for the first time, I was about to publicly disclose my family's trauma in a classroom full of strangers, unsure if they would even care. This classroom represents the "delivery room" for the birth of a story with a tragic beginning but a redemptive ending.

I couldn't wait to take this class. I'd anticipated it answering so many of my questions about one the most important African American figures in US history. When I researched seminaries where I could pursue a master's degree in theology, I visited Fuller Theological Seminary's website and saw Dr. Hak Joon Lee's class entitled "Theology and Ethics of Martin Luther King, Jr." This class and Dr. Lee's background as a King scholar were major factors in my desire to attend Fuller Seminary.

Just a year or so before I watched this film in class, my grandmother had spoken with me about my grandfather and his death for the first time in my life after rejecting my previous attempt at a conversation about him a decade earlier. This was when I first learned how he was killed and that the location and circumstances around Till's murder were so similar to my grandfather's. Hearing the details gripped me. I had this inner turmoil of contentment because I finally had information and bitterness because of the reality of how he died. And now here I was in a graduate course on the theology and ethics of one of my heroes, Martin Luther King Jr., wrestling with the overlap between my family's and our nation's struggle to reconcile race(ism) and coexistence.

After viewing the video for a few minutes as a class, Dr. Lee asked us to break into small groups to discuss how we were feeling and to share our thoughts with classmates. When it was time for me to share, these words came out of my mouth: "I can't look at the pictures of Emmett Till without seeing my grandfather." I had never even thought of those words before, much less spoken them. It was as if they were there the whole time and I was unaware, but the time had come for that statement to be pronounced. I felt this deep sense of vulnerability and empowerment simultaneously. I could breathe after making the statement. Figuratively speaking, I unknowingly had been holding my breath all my life about everything that surrounded my grandfather's mysterious absence. That day, I finally put words and a voice to how I felt about any reminder of his death.

As three of my peers listened to me share in improvisational fashion what I had known at the time about my grandfather's death, there was stillness in the moment. It was as if I was thinking and speaking in slow motion, moved by my own words as they unfolded. As they listened intently to my story, I saw moisture begin to fill their eyes and spill onto their cheeks, leaving streaks of tears down their faces. This was a new experience for me: folks, white folks, were more than interested in my story; they were moved to lament. The gamut of responses ranged from shock to sadness. This was not entertainment that provoked mere pity but a truth that elicited profound emotion.

After a few minutes of our small group conversation, Dr. Lee reconvened the class and requested volunteers' reflections. I volunteered to share what I told my small group. Once again, I was taken aback by the visceral responses of my classmates. They were more than concerned; they had been moved deeply. The best thing about it was that they were not trying to fix anything. They sat in the grief, shock, and discomfort (and for some, I would imagine, anger). In retrospect, I suppose their collective response resulted because in that moment, they were able to connect more intimately to the Till incident of 1954. To have in the room the grandson of a man who was killed in a similar fashion just over a year apart from Till brought all of us closer to the reality of the horror and pain of racial injustice. Suddenly, it didn't seem "so long ago."

It was in that moment that I understood I needed to tell this story. The story of the conflated histories of my family, Black Americans, and the United States needed to be articulated in a way where the dots could be connected between the past and its legacy—our present ethos. It was in that moment in Dr. Lee's class that the word *calling* took on a whole new meaning for me. No longer was I *confined to the pulpit* on Sunday mornings, nor was my message of racial justice and the work required for racial solidarity *prohibited from the pulpit*. In that moment, my voice had been awakened to a broader mission in the world. There was a clarion call to preach the gospel not just in the generic evangelical sense—to save souls by evangelizing—but also to bring attention to the ways that the gospel speaks to the particularities of groups of people like mine who must navigate social structures that produce inequities and injustices.

Just as Abel's blood was said to have been calling out to God from the earth, my grandfather's blood, though diluted with saltwater from the Sampit River, was no longer muted but had been calling out to his grandson to tell his story. His story, and many like it, is the reason we ought to be preaching the gospel. I can no longer circumvent these realities and parse the gospel from justice in such a way that I render it impotent simply because factions of the US American church lack the imagination to see its relevance to forming our individual and collective responses to injustice.

Nate Allen's blood calls out to me in symphony with the spirit to commit myself to redeeming his honor and restoring my family and the community that endured this tragedy to wholeness by telling this story. In my culture, ancestral witness inspires how we live today as well as how we witness back to our ancestors through the same personal and communal ethics. In other words, honoring the legacy and names of our ancestors is central to Black lives. This honor is not intended to compete with witnessing on behalf of Jesus, but it includes the role that the lives, influence, and wisdom of our ancestors play in the lives of their descendants today.

Why We Can't Forget the Past

I heard a politician on a major television news network ask the question, "Can't we forget the past and move on? Slavery was so long ago." It is apparent to me that far too many people in America equate racism with slavery alone, as if the ninety years of Jim Crow following the end of 246 years of institutional slavery and the twelve years of Reconstruction somehow immediately made the nation postracial. This idea that racial inequality is said and done is the result of either historical ignorance of the Jim Crow–era ethos or the discomfort that comes with having to acknowledge the residue of the past in the present. This confrontation of history is disruptive. It is disruptive to comfort. It is disruptive to the idealistic view of America. It is disruptive to many white peoples' self-perceptions when they are forced to concede that they have been passive beneficiaries of an unjust system tilted in their favor.

When someone else posed that politician's question to me in person a few years ago, I remember thinking, and later shared with them, "You evoke slavery every time you say my last name." The name of my ancestors' slave owners was forced upon them as part of the ritual of assimilation and possession by reidentification. I am certain there were no Allens originating from the continent of Africa. I say that tongue in cheek, but the reality is that even the naming of enslaved Africans has its fingerprint on today's African Americans. Erasure of one's name is for the purpose of erasing one's identity. People can't even speak my name, nor can I sign it myself when I write checks and sign contracts, without granting slavery of the past relevance in the present. This thought alone—that like millions of Black Americans, my name once belonged to a slave owner, and now I carry it forever—is disruptive to the fallacious narrative that we have escaped our past.

As my friend Inés said, "An untold story never heals." Likewise, an untold or falsely narrated history has neither wisdom nor lessons to offer the present or future generations. The "untold" only renders us ignorant of our own individual and collective conditions. Without a proper diagnosis of our national status and our real acknowledgment of it, how do we truly heal? The answer, in my opinion, is that we cannot. And we have so much to heal from.

Anti-Black racism—manifesting interpersonally (bigotry), structurally, and systemically—violently disrupts the memory of our ancestors and systematically destroys the whole Black self: mind/soul, body, and spirit. Anti-Black *bigotry*, the most tangible form of racism, desires the annihilation of Black bodies. The architectural design of *structural racism* is meant to control the upward mobility of African Americans by maintaining their marginalization while simultaneously propelling white people to most positions of power and prosperity. *Systemic racism* manifests in laws and policies that inherently discriminate against Black people—doing the work *for* racist and nonracist humans alike—dictating how they navigate the racialized structures. The multidimensionality of racism detaches the humanity of African Americans from their bodies while fostering a collective amnesia that erases Black presence and relevance in US and global history. Not only are Black culture and Black bodies targets in the crosshairs of racism, but the cultural ethos of the United States has also been malformed by this trifecta of iterations of racism.

Some voices from the white community still echo the sentiments that racism is nonexistent because 150 years have passed since slavery. Lynching is said to be a thing of the past, and any incidents of the kind are rare and committed by fringe groups—as if that makes it tolerable. Is lynching Black bodies a thing of the past? In 2014, seventeen-year-old Lennon Lacy's body was found hanging from a tree in Bladensboro, North Carolina. There was overwhelming evidence that he was murdered and his body hung to make it look like the suicide that it was eventually determined to be. There was not even an initial investigation to rule out homicide.[2] In June 2020 there were as many as five Black men whose bodies were found hanging from trees across the country. They were said to be suicides. The lens through which white people see race and racism is quite different from the lens through which African Americans see and experience racism. For example, when an unarmed Black person is shot and killed by law enforcement, we tend to not just see one body; we see the lineage of bodies that ended in like manner over the course of our history in this country. White people tend to see an isolated incident with details to parse in order to see whether this Black person was in the wrong, justifying their death. The difference between the experience of the marginalized or oppressed groups and that of the *group* in power—not so much individuals—is like night and day. White people tend to fragment society in two ways that differ from most African Americans: they subscribe to individualism, while marginalized groups think more communally, and they tend to compartmentalize events, while African Americans tend to see the "big picture" of the series of events.

What happened to Nate Allen in 1953 has continued to happen to African American men and women every year since then. As the main character in *The Usual Suspects* says, "The greatest trick the devil ever pulled was to convince the world he doesn't exist."[3] The aim of today's version of racism and those whose agency perpetuates it is to convince the world, especially white people, that it doesn't exist. The only thing more destructive is to convince its victims that it doesn't exist. This tactic disarmed my family and anesthetizes white people who may potentially be allies in the disruption and dismantling of racist systems and structures.

On that day—December 10, 1953—my grandfather and family experienced several forms of racism: active racism or bigotry, passive racism, and systemic racism. There was the man who shot and killed him in cold blood with his accomplices looking on, there was the woman who witnessed the killing and said nothing, there was the man who wrote "accidental drowning" on his death certificate, and there were the law enforcement officers who did not investigate in order to bring someone to justice. Willing participants collaborated on multiple levels in this web of injustice to seal the lie in the annals of history. This web has never been swept from its loftily perched corner of a structure designed by and for its flourishing. It continues to entangle both willing and unwilling bodies caught in its lacework. Deaths like these, at the hands of racism, have repeated perennially and have also taken on different forms, rendering most white people blinded to their reality today.

Emmett Till became Nate Allen almost two years later. Amadou Diallo, an Ethiopian livery driver shot in Brooklyn by undercover police officers, was Nate Allen in 1999. Trayvon Martin, a teenager followed and shot by a neighborhood watchman named George Zimmerman for "walking while Black," was Nate Allen in 2012. Alton Sterling, a Black man lying on his back with a gun pointed to his head before finally being shot at point-blank range in Baton Rouge, Louisiana, was Nate Allen in 2016. Ahmaud Arbery, who was shot and killed by a white father/son duo while he was jogging in a neighborhood in Georgia, was Nate Allen in 2020. This list could go on and fill the remaining pages of this book. In each of these cases, no one was held accountable for the death of another Black body. To some Americans, these are events we are meant to "get over" so that we can move on. To others more directly impacted by them, they are another case in a history of violence toward African Americans that all but allows us to live, much less move on.

This history keeps repeating itself. Every occurrence pulls back the scabs to the wounds that have yet to fully heal. You can't forget what continues to traumatize you. You can't elude the seemingly omnipresent violence that haunts the color of your skin. Racism doesn't allow you to forget when you are its target. It is like the bully you see in the hallways at school as a kid. You know he is there. You have learned the patterns of how he moves, yet you cannot avoid interaction with him. He has an uncanny ability to camouflage his behavior from the teachers and administrators who do not care enough to notice. You know that at some point, you will have an encounter. There will always be some who watch to see the bully perform at your expense. There will be some who speak out, even if reluctantly. But none will know the extent of the bully's ire like the one being bullied. You never forget the bully.

A bully got to my grandfather that day on the river. He snuffed out my grandfather's life and tried to erase him from our memory. This book is meant to undermine that agenda. This manifestation of the bully left a wife and mother, children, and a community with another void, another hole to try to fill or cover up. Filling the void would take the form of a mom attempting to become mom *and* dad. The cover-up for sons would later take the form of violence and drug use to numb the pain in order to live. But these attempts to fill or cover up the bottomless void live in the tension between amnesia and memory, with amnesia boldly asserting itself. Amnesia about the past produces ignorance about the present, which is its legacy.

More often than not, people prefer to remember songs that bring joy. There is not much attraction to the weightiness of a funeral dirge, since it causes us to recall grief. But there are times when this particular metaphorical "genre" of memory is what is needed. In order to share in the healing, there must be a shared lament. For many African Americans, gunshots become like drumbeats to the dance of lament—which we will discuss in a later chapter—passed on from generation to generation. Memory is embodied in this dance. We can't forget the past. It is part of the rhythm of survival and resilience. If a person or a group of people has never had to dance this dance of lament to the cadence of persistent violence to guns and other such weapons of racial injustice, they will never understand the need to remember. They will never step onto the dance floor but instead hold up the wall.

I recently traveled home to Georgetown to shoot footage for my documentary telling this story. I reluctantly visited the homes of my grandparents. While I walked through the home of my maternal grandparents, I made my way to my grandmother's room. This room has so much history for me. This is where I busted the bridge of my nose while running from my mother, who was chasing me in order to discipline me when I was no more than three or four years old. I tripped just before I reached the safety of my grandmother's arms while she lay in her bed. I believed I could escape the spanking my mother was intent on giving me. Everything goes blank from that point on. A bloody face and permanent scar later, I escaped the spanking and was certain my grandmother comforted me.

This is the room where I sat by my grandmother as she told me stories of her childhood and imparted pearls of wisdom to me. The moment I sat down on that bed with the obvious absence of the matriarch of our family, a flood of emotions began to well up, and I could no longer remain composed in the room that meant so much in forming me. It was uncomfortable. It was hard. It was cleansing. It was a necessary lament. I needed to lament the death of my grandmother. The memories took me on a brief journey and forced me to acknowledge the emotions and release them rather than keep them tucked away in the pockets of my heart until they inevitably burst and spillover. To continue the metaphor, this song of lament was one I hoped to avoid but needed to dance to.

Sankofa

I invite my white brothers and sisters to join in the communal sacrament of "memory" with the African American community. The African concept of *Sankofa* is of great necessity at this point in history. *Sankofa* literally means "to go back and get." It is the intentionality of returning to the past to retrieve its lessons and wisdom to inform how we ought to be today as we move toward the future. History can teach us the most profound lessons if we are willing to seek them out and receive them. In the spirit of *Sankofa*, I pen a part of my family's narrative, which stands as a microcosm of the greater African American experience. The hope is that we may not only learn from the past but also put the events of today in their proper historical context.

I believe one reason for the persistence of the racial divide in the United States is because we do not know everyone's history. As an African American, I was only given the opportunity to learn American history in grade school from a white perspective, but many white people do not know my history. I suspect that many see Black history not as American history but as something for African Americans only. It may be because to be immersed in Black history is to be baptized in the dark side of American history. To learn history from a Black perspective is to risk deconstructing the false image of innocence, benevolence, and morality that many want to believe characterizes this country. Black history challenges those notions.

Then what are we to "go back and get" that is useful for moving the nation forward? To begin with, we can go back and examine the ideologies, attitudes, and behaviors that dehumanized an entire group of people. Deep reflection on these things may help us identify newer, more sophisticated iterations of the very degeneracy that held this nation in bondage. We would be more familiar with the rhetoric or the tone and tenor of the rhetoric that is being echoed today.

Not to deflect responsibility to the perpetrators of injustice only, we would also be able to examine our individual and collective responses, or lack thereof.

For me, *Sankofa* means to go back to a time before Emmett Till to recover what was stolen. Of course, I cannot go back and get my grandfather. However, I can go back and get his name, his honor, what he stood for, and the memory of his presence on this earth. I can go back and get the truth that was trampled over by the oppressive wheels of anti-Black racism. In doing so, I will take my body to places where my grandfather once walked, worked, struggled, and loved. The sacrament of memory requires embodiment. It mandates that I place my body in particular spaces, spaces I once frequented but where I am this time conscious of my grandfather's existence. I can go back and get a part of myself.

Theological Reflection

Jesus tells the story of a man on a journey from Jerusalem to Jericho. While on this road, he was attacked by robbers who were undoubtedly lying in wait for a potential victim. He was beaten, stripped of his clothes, and left for dead. A priest and a Levite headed down that same road one after the other and saw the man lying there. They avoided this man by walking to the other side. But a Samaritan man came along and saw the same man and decided to help him. He was filled with compassion and tended to the man's wounds. He then helped the man to his feet and onto his own animal, taking him to an inn to recover from this traumatic event. He then offered to pay the full cost of the man's stay. He went above and beyond to help this man when the religious folks did not allow themselves to be disrupted by someone in need.

This man who was wounded is analogous to my grandfather, my family, and the Black community. The robbers are the agents of racism and bigotry afflicting African Americans who are simply attempting to navigate this life unharmed because of the color of their skin. The priest and the Levite represent silent and indifferent people in positions of privilege and power who have the means to help but decide not to. More specifically, in this analogy, they represent the American church. But there is another character in the parable who needs to be recognized and understood. The road the man was on was long and winding, and because of its curves, it was conducive to attacks such as this. Robbers could find places along the curves to hide and pounce on the vulnerable. A racist society creates or ignores spaces in its systems and structures that are conducive for racism to thrive. Even though this man was helped and was presumably able to recover, as Dr. King would say in a sermon, the winding road still needs to be addressed.[4] The next vulnerable person traveling that way can experience the same thing. The next generation will have to endure the same violence on that road if nothing is done to make it safer for people to travel.

Likewise, there will be—and in fact, there have been—many more African Americans who will have their murders covered up as "accidental drownings" to preserve the freedom of white perpetrators. Systemic/structural/institutional racism is analogous to the winding road. It is dangerous. It exposes the vulnerable among us who are the targets of agents of power and white racial supremacy—both consciously and unconsciously. Until we change the "winding road" of systemic and structural racism, subsequent generations will continue the hard conversations born out of the pain of anti-Black racism.

Reflection Questions

Do you notice the various forms of racism that exist today besides the blatancy of bigotry? Structural racism? Systemic racism? Cultural racism? Implicit bias?

Have you considered how the past still has an impact on your present as it relates to racism?

What laws, policies, and cultural practices do you know of that exist today as residue from the past?

CHAPTER 2

"Because There Were Bullet Holes"

Rebecca Allen Young

They prey on Black skin
Unsuspecting ones
Suspected ones
Loved ones
But they prayed on back then
Hoping these adversaries didn't violently leave holes in
    Black bodies
Where life seeps out

The Conversation
===

I had stirred up enough courage again to ask my grandmother, for only the second time in my life, about what
really happened to my grandfather. We were driving
home from visiting her son, my uncle "Bobby," who was in
a nursing home. He was only in his late sixties, but because
of neurological damage due to head injuries from his college
and professional football days, he could neither speak nor
move from his bed. He would eventually succumb to his

condition just two months later. She was already saddened by the hopelessness she felt from seeing her son lying in bed and knowing there was nothing she could do to improve his health. I was even speechless after seeing one of my sports heroes in the condition he was in. I call him a sports hero because he was a Michigan State, Big Ten, and NCAA record-setting football player who was in the running for the highest award in college football, the Heisman Trophy, in 1971.

But my grandfather was on my mind for some reason, and I wanted to know about him while I had my grandmother for that forty-five-minute drive back home. So in a moment, the question came out, "Grandma, how do you know my grandfather was killed and he didn't actually drown accidentally?" After all, his death certificate reads, "accidental drowning." This time, grandma didn't get upset. It was as if she was expecting the question and prepared to answer. At this point in her life, she may have been too tired to resist engaging this history. She was ready to talk. She said, "Because when my father [and another man whose name I do not recall] found his body, there was a bullet hole in his body." My response? Silence. Nothing else needed to be said. The depth of the pain she carried was felt in that moment. I knew that what she said to me was the truth. This kind of truth was the kind that was gasping for air while being drowned in silence for too long and came out in dramatic fashion.

I've conducted several interviews for a documentary film about my grandfather's murder. From those who lived during that time and from my father and uncle, I was given the details of his death as they were remembered and shared. My grandfather apparently had an argument with his boss.

His employer was a man by the name of Huskey Cain, described by some as simply a mean person, especially to African Americans. How disrespectful would it have been for a Black man to stand up to a white man in the 1950s?

He decided to leave work that day. It is uncertain if he had planned on returning or if he was quitting the job for good. Someone who worked with my grandfather, an African American man, was told to relay a message to my grandfather that it was OK for him to return to work and that all was forgiven. My grandfather, upon hearing this message, decided to return to work. (I am unclear if it was the next day or days later.) Because he was a fisherman, it was not strange for him to get into a boat with coworkers from the dock just behind "downtown," where stores and restaurants lined the side of the Sampit River. From there, they would go to an area where they would likely be fishing or shrimping. They went to a small island called Goat Island just on the other side of the river from the mainland. This is where the events took a tragic turn for him.

As they exited the boat where Cain was standing waiting for him with a gun, the two white men in the boat tried to hold my grandfather down. It seems from these details that they planned on an execution-style murder. My grandfather, being the great athlete and physically strong individual that he was, managed to get away from the two men. Because he was a great swimmer, he tried to take refuge in the river as a possible escape. Unfortunately, he would never make it in the water alive. He was killed with a gunshot wound to the back of the head or upper neck area and fell into the water as life leaked from his body.

What made matters even worse was that there was a cover-up to hide the truth of his death. One family friend said that the funeral director was told to keep silent about the bullet found in his body. In those days, African Americans would not have dared to say a word about this. They complied because of fear of retribution. My grandmother, my family, and African Americans in the city of Georgetown were left without any recourse for exposing the truth. An entire network that protected white people was against them, and white equals power, just like today.

I was both eager and nervous to learn more, so I followed up my original question to my grandmother with, "Did you do anything to get the person who did it?" She replied, "No. I was young. I didn't know anyone, and I didn't have any money. And unfortunately, that's just the way things were back then." My response again was silence. Silence was the means by which I could process this new information about my grandfather in a healthy way without becoming a ventriloquist for my emotions in the moment. Her response was sobering for two reasons: the first was that my grandmother finally opened up to me about what happened to her husband in 1953. She had never spoken a word about him, and when any of her grandchildren would inquire, she got visibly upset and refused to engage the conversation. I could sense the weight lifted off of her after she shared. The weight of this tragedy had now been transferred to the next generation when she handed it to me that day. I was already in my forties, almost the age my grandmother was when I was born, when she finally had the peace and the courage to share this trauma with me. That was a sacred passing of the baton, an occasion I take seriously. Even as you read this story, handle it with care.

The second reason was because for the first time in my life, I had gotten some details about how my grandfather was killed. For the first time, I could relieve my imagination of its labor and actually know some details of the event that silently haunts my family. In that moment, there was a gamut of emotions flooding me. I felt a sense of relief—even as I took on the burden—that I now knew at least something about what happened. This tragedy was becoming less of a mystery to me. As my grandmother spoke about my grandfather's body, I knew for sure that "accidental death" was a lie. Learning this also made me angry. He was stolen from me. I grew up in my grandmother's home during my teenage years. I would have known him. He would have disciplined me. He would have sat quietly or loudly in the stands at my football and basketball games. I was robbed. We were robbed.

Then as I continued to drive home and process the information my grandmother just shared, I was saddened for her. I felt her pain of losing her husband. I understood the fatigue of having to raise four children on her own. She would remarry some years later only to lose her second husband to illness. Her tough exterior now made more sense. I lamented the fact that she lost her husband, and like many other Black families, there was nothing she could do about it to get justice.

Growing up, my grandmother was tough on me (and others), but I knew she loved me. It was how she loved. She wanted you to be all right and not be without. She likely did not want people to experience the hardships she may have had to endure since losing her husband. This was the grandmother I inherited since the aftermath of the murder of her husband. My great-uncle Henry Tillman, my grandmother's youngest brother, told me that she was a different person after the death of my grandfather. I felt as though the event in 1953 killed them both. He died immediately, but she died slowly until her last breath in 2016. His death was immediate and violent. Her death was slow, methodical, and a different type of violence. She experienced a type of violence that was chronic and persistent over time. It was daily reminders of a new and permanent reality she would have to learn to live with even though her soul was weighed down every day by the memory of injustice.

While I appreciated the context I was given about my grandfather and it led me to grieve for her, the context of the "times" back then made me angry. Like her, there was nothing I could do about it. As Maya Angelou once said, "History, despite its pain, cannot be unlived, but if faced with courage, need not be lived again."[1] This was one of those moments that I wish I could *unlive*. I wish I could *unlive* our history or at least be able to grant my grandmother clemency to come out from behind the emotional and mental cell created by my grandfather's unwarranted death and cover-up.

Georgetown—the Way It Was

When my grandmother said, "That's just the way things were back then," it made me think more deeply about the city that I grew up in, which I realized I never truly knew. I knew during my childhood years that we had inherited remnants of the ethos of the past, but what that past actually looked like and felt like for African Americans were somewhat hidden from the innocent ears of my generation.

I've since learned that Georgetown, like many other cities in the South, had its history of racial violence. Journalist and historian Steve Williams of Georgetown shared some of Georgetown's racist history. There was the case of a thirty-year-old Black man named George Thomas who was accused of raping a white woman. An all-white jury convicted him in 1940 and sentenced him to the electric chair. During those days, whites could freely roam the streets and terrorize Black people with few repercussions. In searching for Thomas, "a bloodthirsty mob of whites cruised the streets of Georgetown beating innocent black youth and ordering them off the streets."[2]

Just a decade later, a man named Arthur "Fat Eye" Waitus was accused of killing a white woman. It has been said that Fat Eye was walking with friends when a white man stopped them and asked them for help moving something. His friends left abruptly, not trusting this man. Fat Eye decided to help him. It turned out that the white man had killed his wife and wanted Black men to help him move the body as a setup. Fat Eye was tried and convicted by a jury of eleven whites and one Black person. His attorney Meyer Rosen made appeals all the way to the Supreme Court, to no avail, citing the exclusion of Black jurists. The trial was moved to nearby Florence, South Carolina, so that Fat Eye could receive a "fair and impartial" jury. Rosen, with a Jewish background, endured slander, ridicule, and vilification by white segregationists for his representation of a Black man on trial for killing a white woman.[3] The town was deeply divided once again along racial lines.

Like so many other cities in the South—and across the nation—during those days, if you were Black and accused of a crime, it was equivalent to being guilty. Accusations need not be met with a high burden of proof. Even in Georgetown, skin color was proof enough. It should be of no surprise to anyone today that Black equals criminal and white equals "the benefit of the doubt." Just as my grandmother said, "That's just the way things were back then." Tragically, we echo the same things today in thought and practice.

In "those days," as my grandmother alluded to, not only was Georgetown riddled with blatant racist acts like this one, but the nation was plagued by the same ethos. Just twenty-one months later, Emmett Till's body would be found in similar fashion as Nate Allen's. Emmett Till was accused of either whistling at a white woman in a convenience store or saying the words "Hey baby." The woman proceeded to tell her husband. Later that evening, her husband, Roy Bryant, and his brother J. W. Milam searched for and found Till at the home of his uncle, Moses Wright. Four days later, they came with guns and threats, taking him away in the night. Till was beaten, dragged to the Tallahatchie River, and shot in the head, and his body was thrown in the river. An all-white jury acquitted Bryant and Milam less than a month later on September 23 after just over an hour of deliberation. Just as my grandmother said, "That's just the way things were back then."

Today, a police officer can choke a Black man to death on camera for the world to witness, and his only repercussion may be losing his job—but only after weeks, months, or even years of pressure from the victim's family or from the local and national African American community and its allies. A young African American man can walk in his own neighborhood and wind up shot dead by the gun of an overzealous citizen profiling him as a likely criminal. This man will be honored with an acquittal of his crime. Nine Black parishioners can be killed by a white boy, and upon capturing him, the police officers will take him to a restaurant to feed him before taking him to jail. I could fill this book with scenarios that will sadden and anger a conscious and caring person to no end. That's just the way things *are*.

The bullet hole in the head, the body in the river, the injustice of white men committing the crime and not being held accountable for it draws the eerie parallels for me between Till and Nate Allen. While Till's death played a catalytic role in stirring up urgency in the civil rights movement, my grandfather's death was the catalyst for provoking pain, underlying bitterness, and anger in my family. I suspect that for at least a time there was the unstable ground of hopelessness that undergirded their lives after this event. My grandfather was a navy veteran from 1943 to 1945, having served in World War II. Not even the status of veteran of the US military could protect him against racial injustice. He risked his life for a nation that saw him as a second-class citizen. He served to protect the lives of the very men involved in his murder and subsequent false narrative about his death. This is the reality of many African American men who served in the military particularly during those days of the Jim Crow era. Veteran status was not a shield of protection to them. It did not afford them immunity.

According to Bryan Stevenson, founder and executive director of Equal Justice Initiative (EJI), Black veterans during the time of Jim Crow were especially targeted for racial terror because they posed a threat to the racist structure that required racial subordination from Black people.[4] Thousands of Black veterans experienced some form of racial terror—from harassment to lynching—after they served their time in the military. There are thousands of Nate Allens out there and thousands of families who have had to endure the trauma of similar events. The idea, I suppose, was for white folks to kill the dream of equality for African

Americans. Military service was a way for African Americans to hopefully achieve a sense of equality. That would not be the case.

My uncle Horace Jenerette served in the army in the 1960s. During his time in the military, he experienced a life-altering traumatic event. He was, what we would call in our cultural vernacular, "jumped"—beaten severely by surprise—by a white officer. My understanding from family members is that prior to this event, he was a kind, brilliant man. This incident caused post-traumatic stress disorder in him. Unfortunately, I only knew him for a short time when I was a young child, but this is the only Uncle Horace I knew; the man with serious mental illness. The residual effects of what he experienced led him to once attempt to kill his mother, Mary Jenerette. He did not even realize he had tried to kill her until he was in the hospital and had gotten his mind back to a place of coherency. A few years later, he did succeed in killing his brother, Frank Jenerette. The catalyst to his mental disorder was racially motivated and event-motivated, embedded into the fabric of a nation built and sustained by racist structures. This is merely a microcosm of the African American experience and a tragic but necessary narrative in American history that must be told.

The Bullet

I often wonder about the bullet. Whatever became of it? Did they put it away in evidence? Did they get rid of it? Did the bullet go through his body and lay hidden in the Sampit River to this day? Or could that bullet have been lodged in his body and actually lay forgotten in his grave alongside his fleshless bones? That mix of copper, lead, and zinc amalgamated to form the deadly piece of object that penetrates bodies, extinguishes breath, and brings destructive and premature closure to life. I wonder about that bullet. As much as a gun is used as a weapon of aggression, taking a life, it is also for protection. Was this man afraid of my grandfather? Did my grandfather represent a threat to him?

But the bullet is not just the material object that penetrated my grandfather's body. Metaphorically speaking, it is also the piercing wickedness of racist attitudes and rhetoric of white supremacy that penetrates any potential goodness that may exist between white and Black people. It destroys the minds of the young white children trained up in its perversion, while it is too often lethal to Black bodies. Much like literal bullets, when the bullets of racist glares, words, and actions are recklessly released in the air and find their targets, they may cause not an immediate death but a slow one. They cause paralysis of one's self-confidence and maturity. They dehumanize one's humanity. I wonder about what ammunition preceded the firing of the gun that took my grandfather's life. I think about the jeers of the crowd spitting on Jesus and spewing hateful words at him before, during, and after the beating he took and the nails that hung him upon the cross. The bullet from the gun was simply the final bullet that sealed my grandfather's fate, but there were many bullets hurled at him prior to that one. He seemed to have lived a life dodging bullets, from the destructive firepower of enemy combatants during World War II to those bullets of racist epithets hurled from the mouths of white men to those of a racist's rifle along the secluded curves of the Sampit River.

Undoubtedly, he had to evade those figurative bullets of hate-filled words. Their only goal was the destruction of his Blackness, even his humanity that once upon a time could have been denied. These bullets have a context. They are not merely objects used in a murder. They are symbols of power. Those with more of them are likely the ones with more power. Those with more sophisticated forms of them are the ones "in the lead" when it comes to power. Bullets were then and still are synonymous with the rope used to lynch thousands of Black bodies for decades in the nineteenth and twentieth centuries. The difference between the two is while the lynching rope produces the "strange fruit" hanging from southern trees that Billie Holiday sang about, the bullet produces the strange fruit that fell from those trees and lays lifeless under their shadows. Or are the shadows those of white men standing over their prey after a kill?

This bullet has decades of reverberations after its contact with my grandfather's flesh. Its initial damage is echoed by the intergenerational trauma (which I'll discuss more in-depth later in this book) experienced by his surviving wife, children, grandchildren, and friends: an entire community still feeling the effects of one gunshot wound. One bullet, keeping in step with the cultural norms of the day, leaves a legacy of death and residual trauma in the Black community. As my grandmother told me the story of how his body was found, I imagine she must have been reminiscing about his body as she last saw it when he was alive, free of a bullet hole to the back of his head. I imagine the internal battle she must have been experiencing in that moment as she told her grandson about the reality of his body having that bullet hole. She must have been arrested by the poetry of the event. She was in the tension of the beauty of how she remembered him to be and the tragic reality of how he was when his body was found.

While bullets are designed for destructive purposes, the bullet holes left behind are evidence of their destruction and much more. Bullets do more than literally tear flesh apart and violently invade bodily organs. They leave behind holes in surviving relatives' lives. These holes are symbolic of the physical and emotional void from the tearing away of a loved one. Bullet holes are analogous to the void brought on by the abrupt and traumatic disruption of relationships by violence. I imagine those bullet holes are symbols for the holes in members of my family's lives, including my own. He was once a husband, father, and son but is now a mere memory of those roles. His absence is the bullet hole in other peoples' lives. His death is a violent disruption of the family and community. Bullet holes are not just the space of torn flesh but also the evidence of physical, psychological, and relational violation and the resulting trauma.

Bullets are unwelcomed projectiles that take life. I've never known of a bullet fired that produced or sustained life. But bullets have no life or will of their own. They are directed by the bloodthirsty desire of morally corrupt—in this case, racist—people who either devalue human life or are in a moment of severe emotional or mental distress. Thus bullets, like the lynching rope, become artifacts of a dark time.

My great-grandfather needed to see the bullet-ridden body of my grandfather to see the reality of how he died. He didn't need more proof of the inherent danger of being Black in the US South. Nor did he need confirmation that Black bodies were not given the value they rightfully deserved as compared to the value assigned to white bodies. He just needed to know the truth. My grandmother needed him to know the truth. My father needed him to know the truth no matter how painful it may have been. I needed him to know the truth.

Theological Reflection

When Thomas, one of the disciples who followed Jesus closely for three and a half years, learned of Jesus's resurrection, he had much doubt (which earned him the nickname Doubting Thomas). He needed to see the hole in Jesus's hand and the scar in his side to believe that it could truly be Jesus who was no longer dead. He said, "Unless I see in his hands the mark of the nails, and place my finger into the mark of the nails, and place my hand into his side, I will never believe" (John 20:25 ESV). Thomas needed to see the scars left behind from the nail penetrating Jesus's flesh. There was something affirming about seeing and touching the scars. Scars and the broken flesh left behind are more than just blemishes in human flesh reflective of injury or death. For Thomas, they were evidence of life. It was the nail-scarred hands of Jesus that were not only reminders of a gruesome death but also proof of authentic resurrected life.

The bullet hole in my grandfather's body, like the hole in Jesus's hands, was evidence. However, this was the evidence not of life but of death. The "lie" written on my grandfather's death certificate would be invalidated by my family because they had seen the mark left behind by such a destructive tool. Scars are also the evidence of trials, hardships, and even death.

Scars are truth-tellers. The mark that the nails left in Jesus's hands told the truth for anyone who would doubt they were witnessing the resurrected body of Jesus rather than a Jesus in spirit. Just as truth is necessary, so are scars. They allow people to trust. No one trusts a person who hasn't gone through anything. People look for scars to know that a person is "real." They want to know that they can relate to them because they too have them. Scars speak the honest universal language of life that we all suffer in different ways and to varying degrees, but we all still suffer and survive.

Scars remind us that our bodies bear the wounds from the rub of humans with each other, with creation, or with systems created by us. Each scar is a word, prepositional phrase, or sentence that documents this language from the margins. Just as Jesus was a man on the margins, navigating oppressive systems designed and enforced by communities of power, so was my grandfather. While I'm not comparing him to Jesus in a moral sense (no one can claim that), the scars on his body are analogous to the scars in Jesus's hands, making him comparable to Jesus in the ontological sense.

At times, God will leave us with scars of woundedness. When Jacob wrestled with (the man of) God in Genesis 32, God touched and dislocated his hip. He walked away from that wrestling match limping. There may not have been an external scar for Jacob to see, but there was certainly an emotional or mental one to go with the likely pain he felt in his hip. He would never forget that moment he had with God. Scars, or woundedness, cause us to be necessarily nostalgic. In a healthy way, it can potentially redirect our memories, questions, concerns, or even frustrations to God.

It is our ethical responsibility to remember. In front of one of the barracks at the Auschwitz concentration camp is a sign with a quote written on it by George Santayana that says, "He [or she] who forgets the past is condemned to repeat it." There is little chance to right wrongs or to confront social issues that exist as the legacy of the past without the discipline of memory. Memory not only makes sense of the present by revisiting the events of the past, but it also causes a necessary grief that moves us to action. Scars evoke memories—memories of that which caused them in the first place. While we ought not to be mired in the woundedness of the past, we must not forget the truth that the past and the scars it leaves behind convey to us.

Reflection Questions

What "scars" have you recognized in people's lives (maybe your own) that are the result of racism? Of trauma of any kind?

Do you know the racial history of the town, city, or state that you grew up in?

Have you understood the legacy of that history as manifested today?

CHAPTER 3

Ever since Then

Phil Allen Sr.

When I met my father he was nine years old
Arrested emotionally
The downward spiral into self-destruction
And the destruction of white bodies
Responsible by association for the murder of his father
Ever since then
He's been searching for him-
Self

My Father's Wound

A friend of mine shared a dream that involved me. Normally, I'm always a bit reluctant to hear about other people's dreams about me, but she assured me that it wasn't anything discouraging or scary. She said that she was attending an event where I was the speaker. Just before I went up to speak, I noticed a young African American boy in tears. I went over to the boy to console him and find out what made him cry. My friend shared that each time the boy broke down in tears, I did as well. This went on for several minutes before I went up to speak and the dream ended. The dream resonated with me because I have a passion for inspiring younger men, Black men in particular. I continued to reflect on this dream while my friend and I continued our conversation. Then it dawned on me that the little boy could represent someone much closer to me other than a faceless, nameless child I did not know. That little boy may have been me, as if the present me was consoling my younger self. But what if that little boy was someone else? What if that little boy was my father? What if that little boy was the nine-year-old who learned that his father was killed seven years earlier, when he was just two years old? What if that was the young boy who never had a chance to know his dad? Recently, my father mentioned that he considered me to be a mentor to him when it came to spiritual matters. Maybe this dream was a type of divine confirmation that the work I am doing through my family's story has healing implications for both me and my father.

I don't remember how my grandmother and I switched gears from her disclosing how she knew my grandfather was killed to its effects on my father. Either I had asked a question that transitioned into this topic or she did herself naturally. She told me that my father found out that his father was killed when he was just nine years old. Her next sentence explained so much about the father I inherited. She said, "Ever since then, he was an angry person." There was a pause on my end as I processed both my own emotions hearing this for the first time and my father's life. I recall hearing such a tone of hopelessness in her voice when she told me this. She spoke as if there was nothing she could have done as a mother to protect her son's heart. She sounded as if she had been living a defeated existence as a parent as it related to him. I could tell she wished there was something she could have done.

I recently had a conversation with my father about what he could remember about his father and how his murder impacted his life. I wasn't sure how he would respond, given the fact that he had never spoken about his father to me in my forty-plus years of living. To my surprise, he was very transparent and candid with me. It seemed to me that he had desperately been hoping to have this conversation with me or with anyone who would care enough to ask the question. I think it was not a conscious anticipation but rather one that from the depths of his soul he needed to have. He began with a statement that affirmed what my grandmother had told me earlier. He admitted to being a very angry individual. He said, "I made it a point to terrorize every white boy I saw." This was particularly true for the white neighbors whose father was the man who shot and killed his father. He wanted them to pay for their father's sins. Why should their lives be enjoyable while his was laden with pain and void because of the tragic absence of his father?

He was so angry that he even threatened a mother who came outside on the porch in defense of her son. At this point in his life, all he displayed was anger. Deeper reflection would indicate that while he displayed anger, all he really knew was pain. Beyond the reality of his father dying by the time my father was two years old, the knowledge of *how* he died was undoubtedly too traumatic for a nine-year-old to process in a healthy manner. Therapy and counseling were not options for African Americans back then. To some degree, it is still a bit of a stigma to talk about personal issues today, especially when the issues simply compound the existential problem of being Black in America.

For my father, challenging white norms became a mission. He grew up to become a young man who defied what was expected of him as a Black man. He shared that when he was a teenager, he would go to the doctor or some public space and intentionally sit in the section reserved for whites. Keep in mind, de jure segregation had ended, but the cultural norms of de facto segregation still existed. His anger led him to be fearless enough to position himself in ways that would antagonize white people as he sought opportunities to unleash his anger in physical ways. Decades after his father was killed, the effects of that racial tragedy kept its grip on my father's soul.

Everyone familiar with my family's athletic accomplishments testifies that we are products of two great athletes in my grandparents. My grandfather was great at every sport he took to, including basketball and football. My grandmother was an amazing basketball player. Some describe her as being a "tomboy" when she was a young girl. Those genes were not lost on their sons. My father and his brothers were gifted with superior athletic ability. They were known as three of the best football players to ever come out of Georgetown. This town and surrounding areas within the county have produced more than a dozen professional football players. Playing at Howard High School, the Black high school in town, they dominated competition under the tutelage of legendary coach Tommy Smith—a protégé of the great Vince Lombardi.

My uncle Nate Allen went on to play college football at Texas Southern University, a historically Black college (HBCU) in Houston, Texas, where he became an all-American by his junior and senior years. He would go on to be drafted by the Kansas City Chiefs in 1971. Later he would be traded to the Minnesota Vikings, playing in Super Bowl XI.

His brother Bobby, also known as "The Flea," was even more dynamic in high school, setting records and wowing the city with his ability to run the football and score countless touchdowns. He earned a scholarship to play at Michigan State University, where he too would be an all-American as a junior and senior. He performed at a level that made him one of the best running backs to ever play at Michigan State, in the Big Ten, and even in college football history. Along with many other records, he set a then Michigan State, Big Ten, and NCAA record on national television in 1971 by running for 350 yards in one game. His college career led to him being drafted in the fourth round of the NFL in 1972. He chose to play professional football in Canada because he refused to play for the Baltimore Colts, who drafted him. I asked him one day before he passed away why he never played in the NFL. He said, "Because the Baltimore Colts were the most racist organization I had ever seen."

My father, who didn't make it to the professional level, was supposedly the best football player of the three brothers. He too played for an HBCU at Johnson C. Smith University. He was named an all-American his freshman year and was projected to be one his entire college football career. He was feared on the football field. He took the anger he carried from the day he heard of his father's death to the field. He played the game not only with great knowledge and athleticism but also with great rage. I marvel at the legendary stories of my father. Even my uncle Nate, who played at the highest level, affirmed the notion that my father was the best of the brothers and was projected to achieve the most as a football player by the time his career would be over.

A Cry in the Wilderness

His career ended at the college level. It was at that time that he and my mother, Vernelle Sherald, would conceive me, their first child. The reality of being a father for the first time was setting in, and he mouthed a prayer that would later change the spiritual and emotional dynamics of his son. My father told me about this prayer he prayed that was reflective of him being in tune with his own inner demons and the fact that it would require a higher power to prevent its intergenerational manifestation. He prayed, "Lord, keep this anger and bitterness and hate that's in me away from my son." It was early in 2019 that he first mentioned this prayer to me. He did not want the poison of bitterness and rage in which he had been baptized to have the same grip on my heart, producing the same fruit of internal and external violence. I will speak more extensively about this in a later chapter.

I was blown away by this revelation. I could never explain why I did not have the propensity to feel and practice the deep hatred of white people as my father had after all I had gone through because of racism as well as all that my family and my people have had to endure because of it. While I am indignant and at times as angry as anyone else when racially motivated events occur, the emotions have never caused me to maintain a deep hatred for white people or any group that perpetuates anti-Black racism. Instead, I have felt the deep sense of grief more than anything for the hate of white supremacy ideology toward Black people and the structural racism baked into American society. There have been many years of my life that I have not trusted white people as a collective, given their consistency as a group to oppress and marginalize people of color, particularly Black people. I've always been untrusting of a country whose culture has been the exploitation of Black bodies largely for the flourishing of white people. I have had moments where I have felt like it would be easier for me to embrace a more militant position toward whiteness. Yet I was always torn by this desire inside to see racial solidarity accomplished in my lifetime or at least to contribute to it in significant ways.

Although my father had the self-awareness to know that this "spirit" could not continue adversely affecting his family into the next generation, this would certainly be the case. My parents' marriage was tumultuous and abusive. I grew up witnessing that anger my father carried taken out on my mother. Domestic violence had been the norm in my home. Very rarely had my father physically disciplined his children, but far too often he took his rage out on my mom. This would last until the summer before I turned fifteen years old. That summer, I decided I would join the rest of my family by moving to live with them in Maryland after having lived with my grandmother in South Carolina for several years. Just a couple of years earlier, my mom and sisters had joined my father to live there. I was allowed to stay in South Carolina to continue playing sports with my friends in Georgetown. A month or so before school would begin, my parents had a major fight. This would be the last fight they would have, and it would be the last time my immediate family would be in the same room, in the same home together at the same time until recently. For the first time, I had separated my father from my mother. This was a type of coming-of-age for me. I finally had the courage to step in and protect my mother. My sisters were too afraid to go to my father after the altercation. I had to try to protect my mom and comfort my sisters at the same time.

The next morning, the arguing and fighting continued. My mother did something I had never witnessed her do before. She had a look in her eyes I had never seen before. She had grabbed the biggest knife in the kitchen drawer that she could find for protection. As the yelling intensified and was likely heading toward a physical altercation, I stepped in between my parents again. My mom was shaking a bit and holding tightly on to the knife. I managed to get the knife out of her hands and convince my father to stay away. For a few moments, he would leave the apartment, and she would get dressed for work. That traumatic event was the last scene of a family that we knew. Violence. Chaos. Fear. Trauma. My siblings and I would find ourselves back in South Carolina by that evening to live with our grandparents, for the most part, for the rest of our youth.

Even at a young age, I often wondered why he would get so angry so quickly and where this came from. It seemed even then that there was this underlying rage that could easily be accessed at the first trigger. My father would later confess that the breakup of our family sent him into a downward spiral of drug addiction, depression, suicidal thoughts, and self-destructive decisions. I had the misfortune of witnessing this spiraling firsthand as a kid growing into an adult. I was too angry with him to see his pain, but I could feel it.

Decades later, my father and I spoke about the recent deaths of his mother (April 2016) and one of his brothers, Bobby (November 2015). He mentioned that the doctor said he was depressed and still grieving their deaths. I listened to what he shared. Unlike the doctor, I was considering the years of drug use and family dysfunction that led to the separation and divorce of his immediate family as deeper reasons for his depression. However, I asked him about what I have long thought was the root of all his pain and rage. I asked, "Daddy, do you think you have been grieving your father's death?" He replied, "Well, Phil, I never knew my father. He died when I was just two years old." I replied, "That's my point. You *never knew* your father." There was this brief moment of silence until he responded, "You have a point there. I never thought about it in that way. You may be on to something."

As a pastor for fifteen years, I have dealt with so many people with deep emotional and relational issues. I understand that the root of many of those issues originates in their formative years from their interactions with family—or lack thereof, particularly with parents. Far too often woundedness from a father's absence, neglect, or physical, verbal, and emotional abuse is the source of many people's pain. While I recognize the "father wounds" I've inherited, I am certain this is the case for my father and where the focus for his healing should begin.

The breakup of the family was like severely pulling back the scab of the scar that was left by learning at nine years old how his father died. The violence was a type of medication for him. It was a way to relieve him of the emotional pain as he consciously and unconsciously agonized over his fatherless reality. Subsequent domestic violence served the same purpose. I believe he agonized over not only the murder of his father but, at the time, the failure of his marriage and separation of his family. He agonized inwardly over the desire to love his wife and children but not knowing how. The drug addiction for decades to come began as a way of "upping the dosage" of what had become medicinal until it served the purpose of no longer numbing but self-destruction.

The trauma from my grandfather's murder had intergenerational tentacles that adversely impacted my own formation as a child and later as a man. My siblings and I inherited a wounded father who never received healing. Although there are many habits and traits that I do not share with my father, there is some overlap. I learned to be a man from a father who was seeking his father. Relational dysfunction in my own life mirrored his. Addiction to alcohol and sex was medicinal for me just as drugs were for him. Alcohol addiction for more than a decade, though seemingly not as severe as his drug addiction, brought about health and social challenges for me. I did not take on the same angry temperament as my father confessed to, but there was still this underlying tension that I carried that could easily be perceived as anger and could be provoked into surfacing. Certainly, like my father, I had little tolerance for disrespect and would easily confront it especially if it was directed at me from a white person—specifically an older white male. I confess there were times I anticipated fighting a white guy for the smallest offense. Fortunately, by the grace of God, I never followed through with it.

The deepest wound that manifested itself in my life was the woundedness from not having my father. For a time in my life, he was there physically but never really emotionally. At other times, he was not there at all. My father was fatherless because his father was killed. I was fatherless because my father was deeply wounded. He had nothing to give me. He had little to teach me or at least little that I was willing to receive from him once I reached my teenage years and beyond. My father's absence from critical parts of my life and lack of consistent and healthy parenting almost undermined the very prayer he prayed over me in 1973. I said to my father once, "I was angry at you. I was angry for you, and I was angry with you." But his prayer over his firstborn would not be in vain. Maybe my father had the foresight to know I needed to be "covered" in prayer not only for more than just anger and bitterness but also for not repeating his habits as well. God would not only preserve my heart from hatred toward white people, but God would also preserve my life from replicating the self-destruction seen in my father's.

For many years, I hit a series of rock bottoms. It began with the end of my basketball career after my last college game. I played on national television, living out a childhood dream. I had previously had several professional scouts from NBA teams warmly interested in me. I did not realize that in coping with a childhood of domestic violence and striving unsuccessfully (to me) to get my father's attention and approval, I baptized my identity in the sport. I needed basketball to validate me, since my father didn't, just as his father couldn't.

When there were no phone calls for tryouts, I dove into what I knew best: alcohol, women, and parties, sprinkled with light use of marijuana. I was numbing the pain with the methods my father (and others in my family) modeled for me. Sure, I could have made different decisions, but this is the mystery of generational "curses." Whether it is practical, spiritual, or a combination of the two, the sins of the fathers travel. For example, I remember the day my father was driving my sisters and me home after the final fight he and my mom had. On the freeway, a car almost cut my father off. My father, in a rage, rolled the window down and began to yell and curse at the man and demanded that he pull over on the side of the road. Without a doubt and with all that had transpired in the previous twenty-four hours, my father was ready to do much damage with his fists.

Years later, while living in New York, I found myself in a similar situation while walking in Times Square. A white man was walking toward me with an obvious intent to not share the limited space on the sidewalk because of the crowd. Just as I thought, he bumped into me without any attempt to avoid contact. He didn't have the decency to say, "Excuse me." I paused, contemplating whether I should brush it off. I decided against that and turned around and went after him, fuming on the inside. I grabbed him by the shoulder, turned him around, and yelled, "You bumped me!" He sized me up as if he was calculating whether he should "try me." I readied myself for a fight in the middle of Times Square. Not only was I ready; I wanted him to take a shot. I hoped he would give me the opportunity to have an outlet for the rage that was under the surface within me. He chose wisely, and instead, he yelled back, "Sorry!" I was satisfied that he apologized, and at the same time, I was disappointed that he did not want to fight. I simply turned and walked away.

A similar situation happened several times while driving years later in Los Angeles. There were as many as three times that I was nearly run off the road or into parked cars along the side of the street. When I honked my horn, the drivers would arrogantly throw their hands in the air as if I was the one in the wrong or even fan their hand at me as if to dismiss my frustration. Again, I drew from what I knew, what I had seen, and what felt so natural. When we got to a red light, I would put my car in park and get out and approach the window nearest me to challenge them to get out of the car. I was ready to fight just as my father was fifteen to twenty years earlier on that freeway headed to South Carolina. I realized how much of my father's temperament I was carrying, and under the wrong set of circumstances, I could become my father in that moment. The same seems to be true of the wounds of the father; they travel as well. In my father's case though, the prayers of the father travel just as far.

I have no other explanation for the radical distinction between my father and me regarding our hearts, minds, lifestyles, and missions than to credit God's faithful response to my father's prayer. I am the embodiment of redemptive prayer.

Theological Reflection

There is something about God's parenthood—namely, the fatherhood of God—that is profoundly important to every human being, whether they understand this or not. Paul writes in 1 Corinthians 4:15, "For though you might have ten thousand guardians in Christ, you do not have many fathers." The distinction made between teachers and fathers is not one of importance or giftedness but one of relationship. Teachers may guide, help one to gain understanding, and correct when needed, but fathers do the same with a deeper sense of love, affection, and protection. Prior to that verse, Paul calls the members of the church in Corinth his "beloved children."

There are many coaches, teachers, and neighbors who may fulfill the role of teachers in our lives, but they do not minimize the gravity of having a father in our lives. My father once said, "I didn't have my father there to teach me how to be a man or to correct and discipline me." Undoubtedly, there were people in my father's life who could teach him, but instinctively, he was not looking for discipline alone; he was also searching for the transforming affirmative love that a son craves from his father.

The results of not having a father there to affirm a son can be seen in Ishmael's life. When Abraham, at Sarah's demand (and strangely at God's confirmation), sent Hagar and his son Ishmael away, essentially abandoning them, it had a lasting effect on Ishmael. He grew up without a father in the wilderness with his mother, having to fend for himself. He had to become a man very early on with no father to guide, discipline, love, and affirm his identity and value. It was earlier prophesied, and one can see why this turned out to be the case, that he would be a "wild donkey of a man" and war would characterize his life (Genesis 16:12 ESV).

One could see father-woundedness in David's life as well; he being the one Jesse would neglect to remember when Samuel came looking for the next king of Israel. He was taken for granted. It would not be a stretch (although nothing is explicitly stated in Scripture) to believe that David felt a need to prove himself to his father and everyone else. He too became a man of war, which would cost him the favor of God that was needed to complete the building of the temple.

While God can parent us in supernatural ways, our birth parents are an extension of God's parenting. God affirms us through them. God protects and provides for us through them. God loves us through them. They actually become a child's first vision of the wholeness of God, as God made humanity the *Imago Dei*; God made them male and female. When children see their fathers, they see the masculinity and the paternal traits of God on display. When children see their mothers, they see the femininity and the maternal traits of God. When one is absent because of abandonment, sickness, divorce, or in my father's case, murder, not only is a piece of the child missing, but a piece of God is erased. In

1953, racism tried to destroy my father (and in a sense, it succeeded), destroy my family, and destroy the image of God.

Reflection Questions

Have you identified the ways in which racism has caused intergenerational trauma in your family?

Have you or family members inflicted racial trauma on others?

What prayers do you need to pray over the woundedness that has stretched generations in your family?

CHAPTER 4

Black *Han*

Phil Allen Jr.

Our bodies have memories unfamiliar to our minds
Primitive
Ancestral
Prenatal
They transcend space and time
They tell intergenerational stories
And the narrative of our bloodlines
Our bodies remember
The lashes the exodus the nooses
But they also remember the tribal drums
The royal dance
Before they raped the (Mother) land

I was raised by traumatized people. My parents carried trauma in their bodies because my grandparents carried trauma in their bodies because their parents carried trauma in their bodies and so on and so on, back to the bend on the African continent in the West African region. When tracing the etymology of the word *trauma*, one succinct definition is a "psychic wound, unpleasant experience which causes abnormal stress."[1] "Unpleasant experience" is an understatement describing the Black experience in America since the trans-Atlantic slave trade. The root word for *trauma* is the Proto-Indo-European word *tere*, which means "to rub, twist or grind, to wear away."[2] Trauma is the painful "blow" that is experienced when one entity (e.g., material, words, visuals, etc.) comes in violent contact with another entity (e.g., body or mind). This contact causes a sheering force that leaves a mark or may cause injury or death. The rotating bullet spun when it was fired as it traveled briefly in the air until it reached my grandfather's flesh to twist away inside and possibly through his body. This is a metaphor for what his murder did to my grandmother's soul and my father's mind. The haunting memories of a husband and the lack of memories of a father, respectively, grind away at their peace. Their bodies and emotions desperately survive in order to raise up a generation whose bodies would carry the same trauma but whose minds would have no idea why.

As a teenager, we would ride our bikes a mile up the street from my maternal grandparents' home to the local store to purchase candy and other snacks. We entered Gene Ward's Country Store one afternoon, just as we had done almost every day during that summer. We couldn't wait to take the short bike ride to the store to play Ms. Pacman and eat all of the Now 'n Laters and Jolly Ranchers we could afford to buy or our stomachs could consume. This day would turn out to offer a different and scarring encounter with the cashier. I picked up a few pieces of candy and waited in line to pay for them. I had a tendency (and still do) to people-watch. I intently observed how the cashier interacted with the white women in line just ahead of me. She had this pleasant disposition and seemed as though she appreciated their business. Maybe they were friends. I'm not sure. When it came my time to make the purchase, I handed her a few dollars. She never looked at me. She did not have the same smile on her face. The softness of her face turned cold and hard, as if she had inconspicuously put on a mask. I'm not sure if this was how she always looked when I bought candy, but this time, I noticed it, and it bothered me. When she gave me back my change, she ignored my extended hand and chose to place it on the counter and slide it to me. It took more time and energy to avoid contact with me by sliding the money across the counter than to simply place the change in my hand. I thought that maybe I was projecting on to her, until the next time I came in and she did the same thing. Only this time, she kept her hand up high and dropped my change in my hand from an unnecessary distance. It became clear to me after hearing from other Black patrons that she had an issue with touching Black skin.

Twenty years later, in my new home of Los Angeles, I had a similar experience. This time, the cashier was not a white woman but an East Indian man. The same exact scenario played itself out. There was the usual cast of characters, a white patron and a cashier. He greeted him pleasantly. He made eye contact. He thanked him. When it was my turn to pay for my purchase, he never looked at me. His smile gave way to a stoic look as he stared past me. I handed him my money and extended my hand waiting for my change. He ignored my hand, and just like that white woman, he placed the coins on the counter and slid them over to me literally underneath my hand. Unbeknownst to him, he had pulled back the scabs of racist experiences I've had. He had poked a bruised and tender wound in my heart, my mind, and my body. I was immediately transported back to that country store where I first experienced the notion that my

Blackness was not to be touched. Something was inherently wrong with my dark skin. Despite the beauty of dark skin from my perspective, some saw it as unclean, like the way Peter initially perceived Cornelius in the biblical narrative in Acts.

The first time this happened as a preteen, I was uncertain as to how to respond to this woman. I guess I was a bit insecure about my own skin. Was it true? Did she know or see something about my Blackness that I hadn't known or considered before? When it happened in Los Angeles, I had a very different response. I was angry. I was incensed at the fact that someone would dare think that there was something inherent about me that he or she should avoid coming into contact with. I said to him, "You won't ring up another customer in this store tonight until you put my money in my hand. You saw my hand right here in front of you. I will shut this store down tonight." I said this at the risk of confirming the false stereotype of the angry, out-of-control Black man. What he did not know was that my response was not just about what he had done but also about what I had experienced twenty years prior. He was receiving the wrath that I couldn't release as a confused young boy.

Both experiences were traumatic for me. One created the initial wound, and the other pulled back the scabs that had supposedly healed over time. What is disheartening is the fact that racist attitudes transcend ethnic background, geography, and time. I was on the West Coast in West Los Angeles rather than the Lowcountry of South Carolina. I was now in my thirties and not the preteen kid looking for a sugary snack between Ms. Pacman games. This time, the offender was an East Indian man, not a white woman. The context was very different on multiple levels, but I recognized the same spirit of anti-Black racism, and I felt the same dehumanizing feeling I did decades earlier.

I remember as a child hearing and witnessing domestic violence in my home. I would hear my mom and dad arguing at each other, usually in the middle of the night (although it could be any time of the day that this could occur). Most times, I could vaguely hear what they were arguing about, but it seemed like each word of profanity was amplified in my child's mind above all the other words they exchanged. It wouldn't be long before verbal assaults turned into a physical mismatch where my father undoubtedly had the advantage and my mother took the brunt of the blows. In my bedroom, I lay with my heart racing, blood pressure likely elevated, and hoping it would end with a simple wish. I could remember my sister coming into my bed because she too was afraid and I represented safe space for her. I would hear a lamp or something heavy fall over and cause a frighteningly loud sound that shook the trailer we lived in at the time. With each sound, there was a corresponding flinch by this nine-year-old trying to endure the night.

To this day, if I ever hear arguing in another room or neighboring apartment, my heart rate begins to increase, my blood pressure elevates, and the hair on the back of my neck stands up as I literally relive the moments of those terrorizing childhood events in my home. For years, I couldn't understand why this happened. Little did I know, this was a post-traumatic experience (I call it this, since I am careful not to falsely diagnose post-traumatic stress disorder). I relive those moments each time intense arguing and fighting occurs near me, and my body flinches at the sound of furniture being knocked over. Sadly, this happens even when there is no arguing. Just the sound of falling furniture can trigger this response from me.

I had a conversation with one of my grandmother's surviving brothers, Albert Tillman, better known to family and friends as "Mickey." I asked Uncle Mickey whether he thought my grandmother continued to carry the wound from my grandfather's death more than six decades earlier along with her disdain for white people. He answered, "I believe she carried [both] to her grave." In other words, he was saying that he doesn't think she ever fully recovered or healed. This is the grandmother I inherited. One scarred in many ways by a culture of racism in this country. Although she was a tough woman and she was not afraid to confront racism at any chance she had, it wore her down over the years. It was an ever-present evil that she and every Black person—whether they were conscious of it or not—had to fight against in order to live fully and freely. I never truly understood what formed her temperament when I was a kid. I now understand, in retrospect. This event was life-altering for her and the rest of the family.

I wished she had talked about it. If nothing else, it may have been therapeutic for her. I could offer nothing more than a listening ear while she released her words and emotions. At least they would not have remained inside, weighing heavily on her heart, her mind, and even her internal organs.

Trauma is an unfortunate reality for all of us. We cannot escape its clutches. It may be from physical violations, destructive words, abandonment, or unwelcomed imposition of some kind that has been inscribed on to one's body and psyche. The word *trauma* is derived from a Latin word that also means "a blow." It literally is the incident, the statement, or the encounter that delivers a blow to someone physically, emotionally, or psychologically. Shelley Rambo, in *Spirit and Trauma*, writes, "Trauma is often expressed in terms of what exceeds categories of comprehension, of what exceeds the capacity to take in and process the external world. . . . [It] is an encounter with death. . . . Trauma is an *open wound*."[3]

Historical Trauma of Black People

The first time I ever asked my grandmother about my grandfather before she was ready to talk about him, I could see her body constrict. I could see her get small right before my eyes. I could visualize the traumatic memories flooding back instantly when I asked her the question about what happened to my grandfather on that river in 1953. Always one to not back down or back away, my grandmother was known to be a tough woman. She had to be tough all of her life. That night, the tough exterior was explicitly for protection. The question I asked seemed to be a violent one. I trespassed upon emotional real estate that had been left abandoned but guarded. This was space in her heart and mind that she had suppressed for the sake of her own well-being. In that moment, with her impulse to shut down the conversation and respond viscerally to my inquiry, she embodied the weight of a community of people: Black people, Black mothers, and Black grandmothers.

I'm going to focus on the African American experience as I attempt to help in understanding collective trauma. To do this, I'll use the story of my uncle Bobby as an analogy to what trauma looks like and how it progresses over time producing a slow "death." Death is not always physical but can also be an unhurried spiritual, mental, and emotional demise.

My uncle Bobby suffered many concussive blows to the head during his days playing football. During a 2015 interview, he recalled having three major concussions when he played for the Toronto Argonauts in the Canadian Football League (CFL). He said when he took those blows to the head, he remembered going back into the game after each concussion. In those days, there was not the same level of concern and knowledge about the long-term effects of concussions and what has come to be understood as chronic traumatic encephalopathy, or CTE.[4]

It seemed as if those concussions had little effect on his brain after retiring from football near the late 1970s. There were no side effects. There were no complications that interrupted his quality of life. Fast-forward about thirty years, and seemingly out of nowhere, he began to show signs that something was wrong. He began to experience headaches, loss of balance, and uncharacteristic displays of anger. But these systems did not come "out of nowhere." They manifested themselves only after the wounds from the trauma had matured and began to show. My grandmother noticed Uncle Bobby began to lose his balance and fall to the floor, once into the glass coffee table in his sister's home. They thought it was a case of vertigo.

Over the next seven to eight years, the symptoms progressed in severity and frequency. His random outbursts of anger often made it difficult to have conversations with him. This wasn't all the time, but because it was not the laid-back, calm-spirited person I was accustomed to, it was both challenging and disheartening to visit with him. The issues with his equilibrium turned out to be more than a case of vertigo. He suffered from neurological impairment stemming from head injuries from years past. He had a fractured skull. The falling progressed to difficulty walking, then to inability standing. The man who once ran for 350 yards in an NCAA Division I football game and maintained a healthy, fit life-style for years after he hung up his football cleats and well into his sixties could not move in his bed without assistance. Ultimately, he could not move himself from his bed. He was officially diagnosed with a traumatic brain injury. His eventual death was due to advanced Parkinson's syndrome and chronic debility with functional quadriplegia.

The injury to his head did not occur in the recent past. It happened decades earlier. Because there were no notice-able symptoms, he was not diagnosed. His physical trauma is analogous to the collective African American experience. In our bodies, hearts, and minds are undiagnosed wounds from the trauma of being Black in a historically racially toxic space known as the United States of America.

The trauma has been constructed by a history of slavery, separate but (not) equal, lynchings, redlining, the fight for civil rights, racial profiling, systematic disenfranchisement, mass incarceration, and the shooting of unarmed Black men and women, just to name a few. For today's African American, aside from direct experiences of bigotry and racial injustice, the idea that he or she is traumatized from events of the past may be foreign. For the upwardly mobile African American, the trauma is even more unnoticeable. Prosperity has a way of masking wounds. It has a cosmetic function so that one may perceive him or herself as having overcome racism or at least being immune to it. Like my uncle's condi-tion, the danger of going undiagnosed for years is that one day when we are least expecting or prepared to handle it, we will get the news and have to manage or survive the disease.

The symptoms are both subtle and destructive. Many families have inherited the residual effects of internalized racism. Unfortunately, too often we have perceived ourselves in the way that a white-dominant narrative that is imposed upon us has dictated. Not to mention the implied messages that a traditionally biased media, unfair justice system, and inherently inequitable education system have predetermined us to be. The fatigue and the wear and tear on the soul for having to constantly navigate these structures have caused many of us to consciously or unconsciously question our worth. When a little Black girl prefers white dolls instead of Black dolls because she believes the white doll is prettier, that is inherited internalized racism. When Black men fetishize over white women, considering them more beautiful than Black women, that is inherited internalized racism. (This is not a critique on Black men who marry white women but rather a specific criticism of those who dislike Black women or consider a white woman to be the "prize.") At some point, we begin to believe the false narrative about ourselves. Self-recrimination is what it looks like to live out of shame, low self-worth, and individual and collective crises of identity. Fatigue then turns into frustration that grows into the persistent righteous indignation that gnaws at the collective soul of Black America.

Black *Han*

This bitterness beneath the surface that we have is carried in our bodies and in our hearts/minds. I was preaching at a multiethnic but culturally white church outside of Los Angeles a few years ago. After service, a white man approached me to thank me for my sermon. He appreciated not only the words but also the tone and spirit in which I preached. He then said something interesting to me. He said, "Every white person needs to hear you preach. I am at the point where I am done trying to be nice and make friends with Black people. They always seem to be angry and untrusting." I immediately understood what he was saying and tried to explain to him why he may have been getting this response. He didn't understand that the attitude was not necessarily a personal response to him as an individual but is the result of a history of trauma that we have had to endure from white folks. The lack of trust is born out of an oppressive history at the hands of whiteness.

He must have been ignorant of the historical pain felt in our community due to living in a racist culture. Clearly he was not aware of our history and how, in many ways, that history is being repeated today in some new and some familiar forms of bigotry and the structures that sustain white privilege at the expense of Black people and other people of color. These connections hadn't been apparent to him. He saw me as "different" from the rest, not realizing that I may have a little more self-control or composure as I preached than many of those he encountered may have displayed, but I feel the same pain and the same anger and am navigating the same systems of racism that they are. He doesn't realize that I may be one encounter with bigotry away from pulling out my sword like the disciple Peter in the Gospels looking for an ear to cut off before Jesus could stop him.

What he experienced with these encounters with Black people was the *han* that has accrued for decades, even centuries. *Han* is a Korean term that represents *the underlying bitterness* that an individual or community carries in their bodies. Andrew Sung Park describes han in his book *Racial Conflict and Healing* as "the inexpressibly entangled experience of pain and bitterness imposed by the injustice of oppression . . . a sense of unresolved resentment against injustice suffered . . . the abyss of the dark night of grief."[5]

According to Resmaa Menakem in *My Grandmother's Hands*, for "generation after generation, our bodies stored trauma and intense survival energy, and passed these on to our children and grandchildren."[6] Our bodies remember well. We may suppress memories in our minds, but our historical experiences are etched in our genetic memory intergenerationally. Our bodies do not succumb to amnesia the way our minds do. Bessel Van Der Kolk was correct in his titular claim, "The body keeps the score."[7] More often than not, we are triggered by comments, interactions, "the white gaze," or tragic injustices recurring in our community. Responses like the ones this man received are means of protection against a representative of who we do not necessarily trust. Our minds and our eyes do not trust because our bodies still feel.

His body feels differently in the same spaces that African Americans have to navigate. His body does not share the same memory. His body cannot recount the same historical data even if he was cognitively familiar with the same history. That history was kinder to him than to his African American counterparts. Until he is able to see beyond his own whiteness, he will continue to ask these questions and be frustrated by the same responses of men and women in darker-skinned bodies. Until he is willing to accept the fact that it is his whiteness (in physical appearance and in way of his thinking and being) that they do not trust, he may position himself to be an unknowing source triggering the pain of their wounds with his attitude, words, or deeds.

Martin Luther King Jr. speaks about the voice of the oppressed manifesting itself in the violence of riots. Not endorsing violence, he is merely recognizing the logical outcome of not only anger without a healthy outlet but also anger persistently neglected by the absence of justice. This violence is not a trait of Blackness but a trait of oppression. When I speak of oppression, I am referring to that which violates and infringes upon an individual or group's humanity and capacity to experience the freedom afforded to every human being. Oppression and dehumanization are synonymous or at least inflict the same destruction upon people. Slavery was oppressive and dehumanizing. Jim Crow segregation laws were oppressive and dehumanizing because they prevented African Americans from having equal access to the same resources and spaces as white people had. Lynching and the threat of lynching are oppressive and dehumanizing, as it does not even acknowledge but seeks to annihilate the humanity of the victims. Redlining is oppressive and dehumanizing to an entire community. Racial profiling is oppressive and dehumanizing because it attaches predetermined guilt on Black and Brown skin. These actions and policies create the content and the context for the language of resistance and even violence. They create the pressure that causes either an individual or a community's implosion or explosion.

I am aware of han in my own life. It surfaces in the face of bigoted actions. It rears its head at the sound of disrespectful and condescending comments toward me or persons of color. I am fully aware that it is right beneath the surface. It reminds me of Genesis 4:7, when the Bible documents God warning Cain that "sin is lurking at the door; its desire is for you, but you must master it." I sit in the tension of han crouching and lurking at my door and the understanding that I have the capacity to maintain composure and not allow it to govern my attitude and actions. I cannot be a slave to han. But I can use it. It can be fuel for my work but not the steering wheel. It can be what incentivizes me to engage both my own individual han and my (Black) community's han while confronting the sources that feed and foster its effects in my life.

I've learned that I have the right to grieve and be angry at injustices that I have learned about, that I witness, and that I experience. In fact, I must acknowledge not only the injustices but also how my own body is responding to and holding onto resulting trauma. For me to neglect this trauma is to be complicit with oppressive forces that target my skin, my ancestry, and my very being. I'm compelled to disrupt the effects of trauma on my well-being as well as the trauma that has plagued my family and my community.

Theological Reflection

Imagine living under oppressive conditions for four hundred years, as the Israelites did in Egypt before Moses received his divine commission to lead the Hebrews out of slavery. Well, we don't actually have to imagine. Just consider the four-hundred-year timeline—almost to the day of the writing of this chapter—that the first enslaved Africans reached the British colonies—later to be named the United States of America—in 1619. This system of dehumanizing servitude lasted for 246 years until the deadliest war on American soil brought about its end. After twelve years of reconstruction following the war, there were ninety years of what came to be known as the Jim Crow era. It was a system of separate but (un)equal existence between white and Black citizens to the benefit of whites and the long-term detriment of Blacks. During this era, the next iteration of domestic terrorism called "lynching" made Black existence, particularly in the South, traumatizing.[8] Redlining made life difficult in other ways, with legal manipulation constructing imaginary barriers where Black people were confined to live.

Following Jim Crow–era laws, dismantled largely by the efforts of the civil rights movement, came racial profiling, which populated the nation's prisons with Black and Brown bodies. What racial profiling also did was create a culture where Black folks are assumed guilty and not given the same benefit of the doubt as our white counterparts have gotten. To this day, laws, policies, and blatant and insidious bigotry have kept Black people at the bottom of many categories as a group compared to other racial groups, especially white people. It has been a four-hundred-year battle for not only equality but, even more importantly, equity. African Americans have been shaped by the oppression of racism.

The Israelites too were shaped by oppression. They carried that han into the wilderness. They had a difficult time trusting Moses. They turned to the forms of gods that they knew best even though YHWH had given them commandments and laws to follow and they agreed. They were a traumatized people while living in and exiting Egypt. How they viewed the world, how they understood themselves, and how they related to God was profoundly influenced by their experience in Egypt. It took supernatural intervention to free them. The same is true for the Black community. I've always pointed out that the slave and the slaveholders who believed in the Christian God had two different theologies about that God. Who has been more faithful to the One True God? I ask this question because these theologies will clash. As James Cone boldly writes, "God is the God of the oppressed."[9] Yet white people invested in the enterprise of human chattel claimed the same God.

This biblical and American history gives context for understanding the source of intergenerational curses. Trauma passed on from generation to generation may be the result of inherited intergenerational sin or effects of the collective sin of previous generations. The sinfulness in the form of particular practices of one individual or group can be passed on to succeeding generations. Likewise, a victimized individual or group can inherit the effects of the sinfulness of previous generations. In other words, the effects of sin upon a group can impact both oppressor and oppressed, resulting in fear, anxiety, anger and bitterness, or self-hate. When the trauma continues generation after generation, it will reproduce the same varied results in those generations. If the trauma is not addressed and the wounds are not attended to, the "curse" from the practiced sin shadows each generation.

Healing social and communal trauma requires first acknowledging and addressing it. The trauma of social sin (or any category of sin) is *disorienting* to people and to entire communities. Repentance from the offending group and acknowledging the wound in the first place begins a healing process that is *reorienting*. But the traumatized group needs the solidaric participation of the dominant offending group to bring forth healing and full restoration of the community. Healing trauma is a journey, not an event. It is a journey that must be traveled by all involved earnestly and with humility. It is a journey out of Egypt, through the wilderness, and into the Promised Land of Canaan.

Reflection Questions

How do you see racial trauma playing itself out in the lives of Black people and other people of color? As a person of color, have you seen it manifest in your own life? As a white person, have you been able to discern ways that racial trauma has played out in the lives of people of color close to you?

Do you agree or disagree with Cone that "God is the God of the oppressed"? Why or why not?

What do you understand Cone to be saying here?

PART 2

Treating Trauma

CHAPTER 5

"Just Let Them Do Their Thing"

On Assimilation and Lament

It will all be OK if I don't feel
If I don't think about it
If I don't fight anymore
But I must feel
Think
And fight
The same way at dawn the sun confronts the night
Because that's what light does
In its radical "otherness"
It feels it thinks it fights darkness and demands space
To be

I could sense how demoralized my grandmother felt when she admitted there was nothing she could have done. She reflected on her lack of resources (i.e., money) and her limited network. Her ability to seek and achieve justice was constrained by the culture of a Christian nation characterized by de facto, if not de jure, lynching of mostly African American bodies. Her hopelessness was what the violence of whiteness hoped to achieve. It sent her back to her side of town to grieve with her own kind so that her lamentations did not make those responsible for her husband's death uncomfortable. Black grief, like Black resistance, is a disruption to the status quo. Whiteness needed her to think that there was nothing she could do about it. It needed her to concede defeat. I learned that all too well simply while navigating my Black body by foot or by car throughout these American streets and institutions.

This was a woman who could do it all. She was a superwoman with the tenacity of a lion and gave you the shirt off her back if you needed it. She was the kind of woman who would galvanize her siblings to go to the local restaurant that did not serve African Americans and stage a sit-in before sit-ins got national notoriety in the 1960s. She was doing this in the 1940s. This woman raised four children on her own and contributed to raising grandchildren and took in cousins who moved to Georgetown and needed a place to live. I thought for a moment, "If grandma couldn't do it, then no one could have done anything." She was the most resourceful, resilient, and tough-minded person I knew. This event in this era with those laws had taken the fight for justice out of her before it could ever catch momentum.

I'm Tired

It was around 2002 when a few of us young men of color were headed out to enjoy the New York nightlife. We were ready for a night of alcohol, women, and parties until the sun came up. Manhattan was the perfect city for the goals of twenty-somethings looking to have fun. My friend Prentiss picked me up from my apartment on West Sixty-First Street between Amsterdam and West End. He pulled in front of my building, and I came out after receiving his phone call that he had arrived and was ready to go. There was Prentiss and another guy, a Puerto Rican brother whose name I cannot remember, in the front passenger seat. I took my place in the back seat, excited about the prospects of the night for meeting a beautiful young lady while having a few glasses of my favorite drinks. We headed east on Sixty-First Street for one block to make a left on Amsterdam and go north for just another short block before we made the quick right that would take us down the street adjacent to the Lincoln Center. This is where our journey gets disrupted.

We see blue lights and hear the sirens of an unmarked police car behind us. We pull over, unsure of why we were even stopped in the first place. We had not been speeding. We were not driving recklessly. The officer approaches the car and asks the driver, Prentiss, some seemingly irrelevant questions but had not told him why he stopped him. Meanwhile, this had been the third experience I had with racial profiling and had grown beyond agitated by these stops and was tired of experiencing them. I told Prentiss to make sure he gets the officer's name and badge number. This was the turning point in the encounter. I could have remained quiet and just let things play out and then go party the frustrations off. But I had had enough.

My statement must have angered the officer. He made us get out of the car and asked for identification. As we were on the sidewalk next to our car, he walked by me and stopped in front of me with a look of disdain on his face. I've seen this look before. It was the same exact look in the eyes of the white kid I played against in a high school basketball game about ten years prior to this incident who called me a nigger during the game. It was a look of disgust and hatred toward my very existence. He stares at me, hoping that I would drop my head or turn my eyes away in submission, affirming his power over me. Maybe his stare was meant to be provocative, enticing me to flinch or move in such a way that would give him a reason to use force. I just stared right back, matching the intensity in his eyes. Maybe my stare was meant to be just as provocative. The exact thought in my head at that moment was "If you didn't have that badge and gun on you, I would drag your ass up and down this sidewalk!" Of course, I didn't say these words. He had no idea that I could tap into almost four hundred years of Black people's slavery, lynchings, and other forms of subjugation at the hands of white people as fuel for physical conflict. He didn't know that I could tap into the rage that came with the reality of both my great-grandfather and grandfather's murders before my life even began. I didn't say it, but I meant it, and I hoped my eyes and body language conveyed that to him. I was confident about my chances of winning the fight if he didn't have a gun on his waist.

It seemed to me that he wanted me to do something foolish. I felt like he wanted me to do something that would justify him drawing his gun and pulling the trigger. This would have only continued the intergenerational killing of men in my family by a white man. After a brief stare down, he said to me, "I can make up whatever I want to and take you to jail, and you'll be in there until Monday." I was speechless upon hearing these words. He was right. He could do and say whatever he wanted, and there would be nothing I could do about it. This was before camera phones or bodycams. I was powerless. He had all the power on that Manhattan street that night. I was speechless also out of fear. I was afraid of this reality. Any movement or comment on my part can be taken as a threat, and his words become reality. He took our identifications and went to the car to run them to see if there were any warrants or anything that he could use to take us to jail.

My attention then turned to the other cop who was present. He was an African American and seemed to be either a rookie or just a couple of years on the job. He looked very young to me. He stood with one foot on the back tire of our car, leaning forward and resting his right elbow on his raised knee. He had his back turned away from me. I looked at him and said, "You know this is wrong. You know he's wrong." Without looking at me he says, "Just let him do his thing and y'all can go." Disgusted and dejected by what he said, I replied, "That's the problem, I'm tired of 'lettin' them do their thing.'" He said nothing. Could it be that he knew in the depths of his being that I was right? I never said another word. I had made my point. I knew there was nothing else to say. We left that night almost disoriented not just by what happened but also by what *could* have happened. I'm not sure if we went to a party that night after all or if I told Prentiss to take me home. Who's to say that on the way home later that night another officer would not pull us over after we had been drinking just because he sees three young men of color in a car together? I realized how easily Black/Brown bodies could attract attention as threats to society.

When George Floyd's murder on May 25, 2020, was caught on video by a pedestrian witnessing a white officer kneeling on his neck while two other officers held him down and watched, it was especially retraumatizing for me. My body had responded in ways that suggested I was feeling a much heavier grief than what the previous killings of unarmed Black people had on me. While my body grieved for over a week, my mind finally caught up, and I began to connect the dots as to why this particular murder was so heavy. It was the police officer's eyes. In this video, when the officer looked in the direction of the camera with a look of arrogance as he squeezed the life out of this young man, the image took me back nineteen years to seeing the same look of hate and evil in the eyes of the officer who stared at me that night on a New York City street. It was the same spirit behind those eyes. I will never forget it. I was triggered in more profound ways by Floyd's death than many of the others. It was the violent look that racist white eyes lay upon Black bodies far too often.

To survive, you almost have to do the impossible and become less Black in Black bodies. You must learn to reposture your body so that you appear to be more "white," which means less threatening and more acceptable. You must be less Black in your thinking and in how you even view the world. Apparently, you must be less Black in your driving too. To survive, my grandmother, in all her pain, learned how to forget cognitively even though her body remembers well. Maybe her amnesia was a way of maintaining some sense of power. Rather than remembering and feeling powerless to do anything, her forgetting undermines the power that the injustice of the event may hold over her. Little did she know, she would enter the portal to a social enterprise that was designed to erase her identity, culture, and history in order for whiteness to advance undisturbed.

The Assimilation Project

In the network 1977 television miniseries *Roots*, the enslaved African Kunta Kinte was beaten because he would not accept the American name, Toby, that was being imposed upon him by the slave owner. In the scene, Toby is heard responding to the whipping with shrieks and cries that normally accompany a whipping. There were tears streaming down his face and shrieks of anguish at every lash of the whip as he endured the public, traumatic punishment. With his hands tied, he was rendered powerless before the dominant acts of subjugation by whiteness. His slave owner was not merely changing his name, but he was stripping away his identity as an African man. It was an attempt to erase a part of his ancestral identity to achieve complete assimilation to "whiteness."

This racial/cultural assimilation project is the violent, systematic annihilation of "otherness." It is the diligent work of white supremacy. I call it a project because it is planned, devised, and has schematics designed to produce a particular result. In the case of Kinte and subsequent generations of African Americans, it is the erasure of Africanness. In one sense, what happened to Kunta Kinte in that scene is a visual, though graphic, analogy of what African Americans and other people of color must endure. To those who are conscious of their "otherness" as it relates to the dominance of whiteness, this can be an agonizing process to live through. Due to the pervasiveness of cultural messaging, everything reminds you of the fact that who you are ethnically and culturally is not of equal value to whiteness. It can produce anger but also a sense of despair and hopelessness that makes you contemplate giving in to assimilation for the sake of peace of mind. Just like the shrieks of an enslaved African man who subjected to the lashes of the slave master's whip, the cries of generations of African Americans are piercing, yet they are a necessary relief. Those cries are in the music, the art, the dance, and the comedy of Black culture. They are also in the rejection of body, hair, and skin-altering products that go underappreciated and often vilified or demonized by whiteness.

The process of assimilation in the colonies for Kunta Kinte and other enslaved Africans aimed to annihilate the African (identity) in them as well as their humanity. In doing so, they had to cripple the African's individual and collective agency. By "agency," I mean the ability to act, to do, and to have the freedom to impose that action or will in any given situation. So not only am I not expected to identify with the Africanness in my African American identity, but I am expected to conform my actions and my agency to that which is accepted by the dominant culture. This is the violent imposition of the assimilation project on the whole of my humanity. That is the agonizing daily reality.

Assimilation has the effect of causing psychological anguish on the one hand, but it can have a numbing effect on the other. One of my favorite films of all time is *Glory*, starring Denzel Washington, Morgan Freeman, and Matthew Broderick. In one scene, Denzel Washington's character, Private Trip, was caught trying to leave the Union army during the Civil War. He was charged with desertion and was punished by being flogged in front of the entire regiment. Trip stared into the eyes of Colonel Robert Shaw (Broderick), who gave the orders to proceed with the flogging. When they stripped Trip of his shirt, his back was covered with whelps from what looked like a lifetime of lashes. The camera begins to pan in close to Trip's face. As he receives the lashes, he doesn't utter a sound. Slowly, a tear begins to creep from one of his eyes, but he never lets out a loud outward cry like Kunta Kinte. To some degree, he was numbed enough to be able to endure the whipping without any outcry. Yet it does not mean he did not feel pain. Inside had to have been excruciating pain. His back was just callous enough to provide a kind of protective coating.

The flogging whip in both scenes is analogous to the assimilation project itself. This is the case because assimilation both is a type of violence projected onto African American identity and agency and has a disciplinary function. The violence of coercively and cunningly deconstructing a group's identity is painful, dehumanizing, and numbing. It disciplines the victims to surrender agency and capitulate to the dominant cultural ethos. Once it is culturally safe to practice any form of racism, even the implicit forms, it gives it the appearance that it is natural. There is danger in naturalizing such an ethos. Whatever is perceived to be natural is likely to go unresisted. It is unresisted because the numbing effect is such that one may be unwilling or unable to remember or to feel the "flogging-like" impact of assimilation.

By "numbing," I mean we are not *supposed* to feel. We are expected to endure and, like Trip, not respond to the figurative lashes of our existential reality. To not feel means to not be human. To not feel is to participate in our own dehumanization. To not resist is to agree with colonial practices and attitudes. It is to live as if our hands are tied and we are powerless without agency. This makes it safe for white supremacy to continue in its traumatizing attitudes, rhetoric, and practices.

To say or do nothing in response to racial injustice is the betrayal of one's own dignity and the honor deserved of those who sacrificed even to death so that our experience today would be a different reality than theirs. Engrained in the psyche of many people is the idea that African Americans do not "feel" the way other people "feel." In other words, we don't feel at all. Because we don't feel, we should not kneel, march, protest, speak out, and so on. In some ways, we have affirmed this fallacy. It is easier to numb oneself like the way Trip did when he was punished. This is a type of side effect of trauma. It forces you to survive by numbing yourself. It manipulates you into believing you deserve it or that you are in fact powerless.

The assimilation project seeks to produce a collective "Toby" and annihilate Kunta Kinte. Toby is more than a name; it is a brand on the psyche and soul of African American selves. Kunta Kinte is terrifying. He cannot be controlled without violence. The language he speaks cannot be understood without proper translation. The movement of his body incites insecurities in white bodies and requires hermeneutical tutelage that suggests a decentering of the white hegemonic interpretative lens. Toby is familiar, even in a Black body. Toby smiles because he is grateful to have what he has from the hands of white men. Toby has no reason to fight back. Essentially, all the fight has been beaten out of him. Toby will not run away. He will not recognize the appropriation of his body and culture. In fact, he will participate in the process.

The Robe of Lament

===

Grandma would sit on the edge of her bed in her bathrobe and rock back and forth in deep intense thought whenever she was stressed. Anxiety covered her like a blanket. She would rock ever so slightly, and occasionally, she would pull out a cigarette. My guess is this rock began in 1953. I wonder if she and my grandfather ever danced that way where she would rock side to side in his arms. The movement of this dance, once a sign of security and love, is now evidence of angst and distress.

She danced to music too tense to put her to sleep. The cacophony of sounds in her life was like an injection of stimulants that abandoned her to sleeplessness. The dance she danced at night when she thought all were asleep and no one would see transferred to the scowl on her face and labor in her gait by day. This is the body language that discipled me. This was what was passed on to me that I refused to carry, yet in some ways, I likely dance a similar dance. It would be like the blues passing the baton to hip-hop. Although hip-hop has garnered global popularity and has become a transcendent cultural expression, its roots are still in the same soil of lament that the blues were nurtured in. No matter how much it tries to escape and replant itself, it will forever be entangled in the roots of its predecessor. It may bear similar fruit. It will even be appropriated—lamentation included—commercialized, and labeled something else, but its essence remains because "they" keep doing their thing. And that thing is what gave birth to this music in the first place.

Even today I struggle with the fact that my grandfather was murdered and my family was traumatized by the racist network whose roots are intricately woven into every aspect of society without us ever receiving any semblance of justice. My great-uncle Mickey was reflecting on the era in Georgetown, South Carolina, around the time my grandfather was killed. He said, "If a white man said you drowned, then you drowned." There was nothing African Americans could do or say to dispute the word of white folks. But not much has changed today. I mentioned earlier the white police officer who told me he could essentially manufacture a crime to take me to jail during the traffic stop on a New York City street corner. He merely echoed the words of his predecessors before him, and together, we reenacted countless racist encounters between whites and African Americans with white people projecting their fears and/or their power onto vulnerable Black and Brown skin.

Intergenerational lament is a result of not only the grief that has been passed on from within the African American community but also the actions and ideology that have been passed on within the white community and imposed upon African Americans that perpetuate this phenomenon. What my grandmother and my great-uncle experienced in the 1950s, African Americans experience today. The tragedy reconfigured my grandmother's being. It crippled my father. Both the lament I inherited and the racism that still breathes today has had a role in forming me. My body has known even when I was not cognitively aware. My grandmother's body knew. My father's body knew. The collective body of the African American community (and I suspect other communities of color) has known since the first enslaved African's feet touched the soil of Jamestown, Virginia.

When my grandmother rocked back and forth, it was a rhythm of lament and one preparing to fight. Like the athlete that bounces around warming up his or her body before game time or the boxer who emulates his or her movement in the fight that is about to ensue, she was rocking in preparation to fight off apathy and despair. But like a baby in her mother's arms after a fall that left a bruise on her knee, she rocks, seeking the safe space of solace to settle her spirit from the trauma that wounded her in 1953. They cannot just keep doing their thing. Their "thing" is violent. Their thing disciplines our whole lives and touches the deep crevices of our souls. They no longer have permission to keep doing their thing.

Theological Reflection

Assimilation is not just an erasure of a minority group's ancestral and cultural identity. It is also an affront to the creative and providential work of God. Biblically, God is responsible for both the mandate and the initiation of cultural diversity. Part of the Divine command in Genesis 1:28 was that humanity, beginning with Adam and Eve, would "multiply and fill the earth." In essence, God's desire was that God's image would be replicated and spread throughout creation. In Genesis 11 after God flooded the earth in an effort to cleanse it of humanity's sinful ways up to that point, creation underwent a type of baptism, and there was a dispersal of the Shinarites throughout the earth. This diversity in culture was pioneered by God's providential hand confusing the language of a group of people who desired to build a tower that could reach the heavens. This planned act fueled by hubris and human inclination for autonomy displeased God, and God responded by confusing their language, which caused them to disperse throughout the earth. This was the antiassimilation act of God. The intentional systematic dissolution of diverse cultural expressions into one is ungodly and secular at its core. By "secular," I borrow from Vincent Lloyd in *Race and Secularism*, where he defines it as "a desire to stand outside religion . . . evok[ing] a religious domain that is managed by power and that is circumscribed by non-religious forces."[1] Human pride, by nature, is anthropocentric and seeks to govern creation on its own terms. This is also true of cultural assimilation.

Assimilation is not just the annihilation of a group's identity, but it also involves the nullification of moral agency. Whether one chooses to ascribe terms such as *tyrannical, imperialistic,* or *colonizing,* assimilation is an attempt to dictate the agency of the minoritized "other." Daniel, along with Shadrach, Meshach, and Abednego, were taken into exile, as most of the Israelites were at the hands of Nebuchadnezzar. From the time he was a teenager to when he was at least eighty years old, Daniel faced the boldness and forcefulness of assimilation. As a teenager, Daniel defied the Babylonian custom of eating meat sacrificed to the king. Some years later, Nebuchadnezzar made a golden image and required that everyone in the land would bow down and worship at an appointed time. Shadrach, Meshach, and Abednego resisted the decree to worship the image even in the presence of the king. Daniel, now around the age of eighty, disobeyed an ordinance that forbade anyone to make petitions to any god besides King Darius. The four Hebrew boys-turned-men resisted the imposition of the secular, that which stood outside of religion (as it relates to their God) and centered on Babylonian customs and deities.

In the midst of the seventy years of resisting conformity to the Babylonian culture, they waited. They had no power. They had no resources other than what may have been given to them. Their only hope was in YHWH. They lived at the intersection of assimilation, powerlessness, and faith, knowing the God of the universe is the source of their power and security and survival.

This is the same intersection that the followers of Jesus felt when witnessing and hearing about the reality of his undeserved execution. Their experience was more of a theological reassimilation away from the "Way" and a return to orthodox Jewish thought and practice. Many hid, some watched from afar, but none had the resources or the capacity to stop neither what was happening nor the persecution that ensued because they held steadfast to their testimony regarding the truth about Jesus as the Son of God come to save the world.

Forced or manipulated assimilation, even in a religious context where one attempts to evangelize and disciple, is not a characteristic practice of God. When the Jewish disciples refused to continue to follow Jesus—the one who offers eternal life—he did not force them into a relationship that would certainly lead to transformation and a renewed worldview. In John 6, Jesus allows them the freedom to walk away and to keep their cultural and religious identities intact. Assimilation—the process of becoming like something else—is done by the Holy Spirit and is not a coercive act but one that guides, leads, and draws one into change. However, even in this metamorphosing process, one's identity is not diminished but brought to the fore as a part of the reflection of who God is. The same Spirit fortifies human agency. In other words, the work of the Spirit reinforces one's humanity—including the particularities—rather than deprives one of it.

Reflection Questions

In what ways have you seen or experienced and felt the violence of cultural assimilation due to living in a racialized society dominated by "white" culture?

What function can the Holy Spirit play in empowering those who are subject to assimilation?

What do you think has to happen to spur society, especially the church, to engage in antiracism (or anti-assimilation) so that racism no longer has safe spaces to exist or even flourish?

CHAPTER 6

A New Prescription

On Healing Black Trauma

You pretend well
You pretend not to see my skin
Not to hear my voice
Not to discern my pain
Your privilege affords you that choice
You pretend that you transcend
The fragile construction you created
But in fact you aren't deaf and blind
Because the trajectory of your ropes and bullets over
    time
And the oppression of your legislative pen
Say otherwise

The smile on my face and presenting myself as less threatening doesn't heal the constant disorientation my body feels. In fact, it is quite painful to have to put on the smile. It is exhausting consciously showing up in the less threatening version of myself. This method of coping is no more successful than my father demonstrating his rage by fighting white boys in the neighborhood when he was growing into manhood. My father attempted to fight his way out of the disorientation only to exacerbate his situation. The stress level that comes with that degree of rage is crippling. I know this because I witnessed the manifestation of that rage imposed upon my mom physically and verbally. I felt that rage reverberate through the walls to arrest me in my bed at night. Two generations and two methods of coping but having the same result of disorientation navigating white spaces in Black bodies. There has got to be an alternative way. And healing cannot be my responsibility alone.

As an athlete, I developed this tendency to experience an injury or a health concern and respond by "toughing it out." Recently, I experienced a moderate level of abdominal pain. Given the fact that I am typically a healthy person, I did not think much of it. I figured it would simply fade away. My injuries pale in comparison to the chronic traumatic encephalopathy (CTE) my uncle Bobby experienced as a college and professional football player. One day in a conversation with me, he told me about those major concussions he suffered while playing in the CFL. For most of his life, he was one of the healthiest people I knew until one day he began to lose his balance and fall unexplainably. When I asked about the loss of balance and the falls, he told me it was a severe case of vertigo.

Further examination revealed the fracture in his skull and CTE—which led to the diagnosis of Parkinson's disease. I am not sure if it was possible that he could have been healed from this disease barring divine intervention, but I do know that the treatment he initially received would not have matched the diagnosis. What can be more counterproductive than treating the wrong illness? Falsely diagnosing my uncle with vertigo rather than the brain injury may have given him a false sense of security that rest, medicine, or some treatment could resolve the issue so that he could continue on with his life.

My uncle's health concerns leading to his death in 2015 are analogous to the social experience of my family in particular, the African American community more broadly, and people of color in general. The slight fracture in his skull and corresponding brain injury went undetected for many years, yet even in the nascent stage, these twin injuries were becoming progressively crippling to his health. The construction of race has been a chronic social disease that produced the perceived fissure between Blackness and humanity, between "otherness" and divine image-bearing. No matter how obvious racialization has been in plaguing US and even global society, there is a conscious and unconscious denial of the disease of racism. The false notion that the United States is a postracial culture particularly because of the reality of an African American president is as dangerous a prognosis as the erroneous diagnosis of vertigo to explain my uncle's neurological impairment.

How can we ever expect to heal as a nation from the chronic inflammation of a cultural evil that continues to affect all of us if we never get diagnosed or if we never acknowledge the diagnosis? How do we treat a disease when the extent to which we are willing to describe it is that it is a generic illness (if we are willing to identify it at all)?

The typical response given by far too many white evangelical Christians is that it is just sin. In saying this, what they mean is that there is nothing distinct about racism from any other sin that everyone has to experience. They are correct in saying that it is sin, but what they do not appreciate is how pervasive, imperceptible, and pernicious racism is. Generally, there is no acknowledgment or deep understanding of systemic/structural/institutional racism. For many, blatant bigotry is the extent of their understanding of racism. They grasp only what they can see. The forms of racism that are insidious and imperceptible go unnoticed and thus dismissed. By and large, most people would identify the shooting of my grandfather as a racist act. But many will not include the signing of the death certificate that contains the lie of "accidental drowning" as a form of racism. They may give the benefit of the doubt to law enforcement who did not investigate the crime. They may even empathize with the woman who saw two men struggling with my grandfather just before he was shot and killed. There was testimony that went to the grave untold.

This generalization of sin is being challenged in the United States and around the world following the cluster of murders of Ahmaud Arbery, Breonna Taylor, and George Floyd. After years of pleading the case for systemic issues in law enforcement involving policing Black people unjustly, the country is in an uproar and has been forced to see what Black people have known all along. White people, unless they stubbornly choose to, can no longer say this is a rare occurrence. Even the NFL has publically admitted that they were wrong to ignore the systemic anti-Black racism that exists not only in law enforcement but throughout US society.[1]

As a Christian, I believe that Jesus is God's redemptive response to all sin, but Jesus's life, ministry, and teachings also speak to the particularities of sin. The same should be the case for the Christian perspective and response to sin in its particular manifestations today even though it is apparent that factions of the church have failed at this. It would not be wise to just give someone who is sick with the novel coronavirus (COVID-19) any drug that has addressed other types of viruses in the past. This particular virus must be examined and the drugs trial-tested before administering them to the patient. In other words, particular viruses generally require particular vaccines to be developed. It would be irresponsible to give a cancer patient medicine intended for heart disease even though the cancer patient and the person with heart disease are both sick. In these analogies, the patient is America and the sickness is ~~racism~~ white supremacy. What's left is to identify the appropriate medicine.

Drug of Choice

If we closely examine the United States metaphorically as a "patient," we will see that there are two types of medicines being consumed. White people have one kind of medicine or drug and people of color—namely, African Americans—are taking another kind. For many white people, amnesia and color-blind theology/ideology apparently have medicinal qualities. The ethic of forgetting the past is a way to alleviate the weight of the collective shame from a history of racial oppression. Even though many white people today do not actively participate in racist practices, they understand that it was their ancestors and their racial-ethnic group(s) that perpetuated such heinous acts creating a culture they would tolerate. Some even understand that while they are not active participants, they do benefit from a system and a society designed for those with white skin. Others are aware that this social structure marginalizes people of color and in many ways targets African Americans with its anti-Black sensibilities.

Besides being deaf and blind to the past, they perceive that there are benefits to color-blind theology/ideology. Color blindness is the idea that one does not, nor should one, see skin color. To acknowledge skin color from this philosophical standpoint is counterintuitive to the idea of eradicating racism. To them, any preoccupation with skin color and other ethnic features undermines those efforts even though a racialized culture is by nature preoccupied with color. It is really a preoccupation with "otherness." Foundational to American society and dating back to European encounters with Native people is the perverse view of non-white ethnicity subjected to the supremacy of whiteness. This ideology is woven into the fabric of American systems and structures. This is what color blindness is trying to avoid. It is a feeble attempt to provide an escape route from the ideology of white supremacy over people of color. In this thinking, a person is not accountable for what they do not see.

There are some drugs that are more expensive than others, and some people can only afford the less costly version. African Americans cannot afford the medicines of amnesia and color blindness. They are too costly to Black existence. Yet for white people, they represent the generic or the less costly medicine for the disease of white supremacy. Racialization depends on the "otherness" of color and physical features that deviate from the white norm. Therefore, existentially, African Americans are bound to the constant awareness of skin color. There are African Americans who choose to forget or claim color blindness with the hopes that they can escape being victimized by racism or be accepted by the white community as one just like them. But this is only successful up to the point that they or someone close to them experiences bigotry or any fruit of systemic/structural/institutional racism. The criminal justice system and the disparities in arrests, sentencing, and imprisonment between African Americans (and Latinos) and white people remind us of color. The inequities in funds allocated to schools made up of predominantly white students versus schools of color remind us of color. The embarrassing and glaring absence of people of color in CEO positions for Fortune 500 companies reminds us of color. The fact that African Americans can make up the majority of athletes in professional and collegiate basketball and football yet have minimum representation in coaching, executive leadership, school athletic director positions, president positions, and ownership roles reminds us of color.

Our medication has taken many forms over the years. Much like my grandmother and father, refusing to voice and name the trauma from racism has been a coping mechanism for African Americans. It's as if not speaking of the tragedies that have plagued our community is therapeutic. For that reason, the African American community has passed on secrets along with trauma to succeeding generations more than we have passed on healing methods. To give voice to the reality of the trauma carried in our bodies is an empowering step toward healing for any marginalized community. This is why hip-hop (though not perfect) and other genres of Black music became such a powerful and prophetic cultural expression. It audaciously gave voice to the Black experience. The art of storytelling through literature, art, and film projects—*Roots* (1977), *Beloved* (1998), *12 Years a Slave* (2013), and *When They See Us* (2019)—serves to function as more than entertainment; it serves as platforms for African Americans to see themselves in their own narrative and hear their stories in their own voices.

Another costly form of medication for African Americans has been the internalization of racism. This is not so much a conscious decision as much as it is an unconscious one born from perpetual subjugation to racist cultural messaging. If a person sees enough negative images, is exposed continually to communities stripped of vitality because of racist policies, and fails to be exposed to his or her own people's contributions to society, then at some point, that messaging is believed and internalized. It becomes easier, even more natural and rational, to stop fighting a losing battle and simply give in and echo the messaging. This may manifest itself in the "vandalization" of the African American community already depleted of resources. It may result in gang membership, seeking belonging, identity, and safety in an environment that fails to provide any of those things. It may also result in assimilation to whiteness because of a hatred of the image that the Black self projects. The medications, in these various forms, are not stimulants, but they are depressants that have the potential to retard our moral agency in seeking justice while resisting all forms of racism.

Conversely, what is *needed* from within the African American community in order to counter the effects of internalized racism is affirmation and empowerment through education, storytelling, and mentorship. Internalized racism is only successful where the individual or group is ignorant of the truth—when the African American community's stories are told for the people and distorted in ways that attempt to eternalize fallacies that attach meaning to selfhood. To be clear, this is not new to the African American community, but more is needed both within and beyond the African American community to educate others while at the same time dispelling untruths that foster and justify racist attitudes, policies, and actions. The platform for African Americans must expand beyond the African American community.

When a group's perspectives and stories are mainstreamed and amplified in the public sphere, it serves as validation. They begin to internalize the affirmation of selfhood rather than the racism that has had intergenerational effects in the formation of the individual or collective Black self. When African American youth heard the hip-hop classic "The Message" by Grandmaster Flash and the Furious Five, it was more than a cool song on the radio; it was their stories and their realities being broadcasted to the world. Their reality may have depicted the despair and harshness of urban living at that time, but they were being heard and, more importantly, seen. The same can be said for films, like *Black Panther* (2018), that depict Blackness with the dignity, regality, and innovation that our African ancestors once represented.

For the deconstruction of internalized racism, it is important that we own our storytelling. Stories about African Americans told from the African American perspective contain the details, the pain, the layers, and the soul of the experience. The authenticity of the vernacular—the "mother tongue"—of the community resonates. When I say "mother tongue," I am talking about the everyday lingo—literally and figuratively—that naturally flows off the lips of Black people. Once again, seeing and hearing our stories told from our voices is affirming of Black selfhood. Our stories have a particular rhythm, a recurring sequence of events[2] that requires intimate knowledge and sensitivity for the sake of accuracy and impact. Storytelling inspires storytelling. If one person's story matters, then so do others' stories. For example, when I produced the documentary short film *Open Wounds* (2019) that corresponds with this book, I screened the film in my hometown of Georgetown, South Carolina. After the screening, during the Q&A session, African Americans in attendance began to share similar stories of families who have experienced the same tragedy as my family had. The rhythms of being, suffering, resiliency, redemption, and healing are embedded in the Black experience and can only be captured by African American storytellers and historians. The proofreading of written and dramatized accounts of our history—our story—is necessary for the empowerment, validation, and affirmation of each generation in our community.

Internalized racism is further deconstructed by mentorship. When I speak of mentorship, I am referring to what a friend of mine describes as life-on-life ministry. It is the model that Jesus gave us. It is what was once common for many coaches and teachers who believed that it truly takes a village to raise a child. Mentors have saved lives. What this says to a child (or to adults) is that they are seen and they are loved because they matter. Words and deeds of affirmation over time can penetrate the toxic internalization of racism. Mere presence through the patient investment of time can reverse the effects of internalized racism and resurrect the life that had been drowning in the murky, racist-infected waters that too many African Americans have had to swim in. The appropriate prescription is not to blind ourselves or to forget (white people), nor is it to remain silent and internalize the experience with racism (African Americans), but to see, speak, and invest in its deconstruction.

Trump-Era Relapse

When someone has an addiction of some kind, it is said that they are struggling with a disease. They have a sickness that requires detox, therapy, discipline, and boundaries. If they are willing to adhere to these rules and principles, they will be successful in achieving sobriety and maintaining good health. If they violate any of these principles, they are susceptible to relapse. Racism is a social disease, and to a greater degree, whiteness is the disease of identity. While it fails to acknowledge and respect the dignity of African Americans, it has already achieved annihilation of the identity of those of European descent. There is disturbing allegiance to the term *white* as an identity marker. Many white people struggle to detach themselves from this label, as there has not been offered a sufficient alternative. This allegiance remains intact even though race, whiteness, Blackness, and so on are all fruit of racist ideology.

In the years during the first African American presidency under Barack Obama, there was a sense of racial hope for all Americans and certainly racial pride for African Americans. This rise in empowered voices and agency from African Americans inspired by seeing themselves in the Obamas, occupying the highest office in the land as well as the changing racial landscape, was apparently disruptive to many white Americans. The number of hate groups rose to record-level highs during the Obama administration.[3] This rise in hate groups continued under the current Donald J. Trump administration. The rhetoric from the highest office in the land gives license for hate groups to come even further out of the shadows. "Make America Great Again" is more than a presidential campaign slogan. For some, it is a clarion call to the white hate groups on the fringes to reclaim *their* America even if it came in the form of "dog-whistling." It is no coincidence that this is the atmosphere that followed the radical reality of an African American president.

"Make America Great Again" further inspired a social relapse back into the dark side of the nation's history. Racists are once again emboldened to make their presence known and to assert their ideologies in the public discourse around race. These ideologues, whether neo-Klansmen or politicians (or the same individual in some cases), always center whiteness and vilify people of color as posing threats to America's "greatness." This era under the Trump presidency has awakened the zeal of defending whiteness at all costs, even at the cost of Black and Brown lives. There are distinctions and similarities between this era and the 1950s pre–civil rights movement. The similarities are the countless murders of African Americans at the hands of white people and few instances of justice prevailing in holding the killer(s) responsible. The difference today is that technology has allowed us to capture heinous crimes against our humanity (e.g., Rodney King, the Charleston Nine, and Philando Castile) for evidence and public consumption. Whiteness is the substance being abused. It is what many in the white community have relapsed on.

When I speak of whiteness, my understanding is informed by Willie Jennings's definition of it being a "deformed building project (formation) aimed at bringing the world to its full maturity."[4] Love Sechrest and Johnny Ramirez-Johnson identify in Jennings's work that whiteness functions to order "global systems of dominance that favor Whites and that have in turn *nurtured racism, white supremacy,* and patriarchy."[5] The nostalgic call to "Make America Great Again" conjures up euphoric feelings of a time when whiteness went largely unchallenged, as in the case of my grandfather's death. Whiteness put fear in people's hearts, like the funeral director or the supposed eyewitness who saw my grandfather struggling with two white men before he was shot and who could have spoken out about the truth. Whiteness decided there was no need for an investigation. Whiteness preserved the freedom of the man who killed my grandfather living just a few doors down from my family. Whiteness is the drug. Many in the white community are the addicts who have relapsed. Like a drug house where dealers and addicts alike frequent, this Trump-era political climate facilitates the environment for a return to a traumatic past.

Setting a New Table

Historically, white Americans have had the controlling seat at the "table" of any discourse. Whether it's political, economic, or social, the narratives are generally controlled by white voices. People of color, particularly African Americans, may get a token seat at the table. We can remain at the table as long as we "behave." By "behave," I mean *not* disrupt the dominant narrative in progress regardless of its inaccuracy, insufficiency, or offensiveness. There is a prescription that is transracial in its implementation and requires participation from African Americans and white people. It will require a new table with new table setters.

African Americans as well as all people of color must be willing and able to set their own "table." At this table, we control the narrative. At this table, we send out the invitations. The playing field has been leveled by innovations in technology, such as social media. However, at this table, white people must be willing to accept the invitation. They must be willing to accept the invitation and relinquish their power. It is not so much reverse tokenism, but instead, it is simply the inverse of the prevailing structure that inadequately confronts racism in its totality. This is the table where white people must be willing to defer to the authoritative voices of communities of color. In fact, communities of color hold the authority when it comes to addressing racism, as our lives have been violently shaped by it.

"Setting the table" is providing the space where we tell our stories and brainstorm the solutions, albeit collaboratively. It is a space where whiteness must defer its hegemonic ordering to voices from the margins. We must consider more deeply the lessons offered by the scene of the Last Supper. Jesus was a marginalized poor carpenter under duress from Jewish leaders threatened by the influence of his ministry and teaching. He lounged around the table with young unlearned men, sharing a meal and wine. Oppressive power would not have been welcomed at that table. Only those who would have been willing to demonstrate dependence upon the Divine and interdependence upon brothers and sisters could find a place at the table. It is a space of the prophetic—"behold the hand of him who betrays me is with me on the table" (Luke 22:21). This is a space of lament—"this is my blood of the covenant . . . poured out for many for the forgiveness of sins" (Matthew 26:28). This is a space of (eschatological) hope—"when I drink it new with you in my Father's kingdom" (Matthew 26:29). This is the space of solidarity.

Theological Reflection

We have forced God's hand to see color. Revelation 7:9–17 describes a scene of many people from every nation and culture before the throne in a collective posture of worship. Many Christian pastors use this text to underscore color-blind theology. Because there will be a multicultural presence in worship where socially constructed frameworks, like race, will not matter, they encourage us to begin to think that way now. Multiethnic ministries are built on this premise. At the same time, these pastors and churches remain silent, often turning a blind eye to social injustices that persist in American society and beyond. This theological position is problematic because we do not live in that reality visualized in Revelation 7. We live in a world where the color of one's skin, the texture of one's hair, the width of one's nose, or the fullness of one's lips have had meaning attached in ways that falsely measure the worth of an individual or group.

We must consider what Jesus said in Luke 10 in the story of the Samaritan man. Jesus purposefully identified the ethnicity of the man who helped another man who was beaten and left for dead on the side of a dangerous road. He intentionally exposed the ethnic background of the men who walked to the other side of the road in order to avoid the dying man by naming them "the priest" and "the Levite." Knowing the tension between the Jews and Samaritans, Jesus was making a point by distinguishing not only the men's ethnicities but also their ethical choices. Jesus, a Jew himself, praised the supposed enemy, the Samaritan, while apparently critical of his fellow Jewish brothers, the priest and the Levite. Jesus wanted his audience to recognize the ethnicities. Their backgrounds mattered in the context of the adversarial relationship between the two groups.

We have constructed ideologies in our minds and systems and structures that oppress and marginalize based on racial/ethnic background. These constructions have been passed on oftentimes uninterrupted and unmodified to be inherited by generations that receive them as natural. So oppression and marginalization seem natural and are far too often uncontested. In addition, they are defended. Color-blind theology in the midst of this reality is ungodly. God does not see a disembodied human with universal features. God sees every detail, every mark, and every hair on one's head. God sees all that makes a person who she or he is. In fact, as God sees color, other physical features, and ancestry, God places value on these. None of these attributes of a person diminishes the worth of the image-bearer.

Reflection Questions

In what ways do you think the post-Obama era impacted race/racism?

What does "Make American Great Again" mean to you? Do you think the statement has racial undertones? Why or why not?

Do you subscribe to color-blind theology? Why or why not?

CHAPTER 7

A New Prescription

On Healing White Trauma

Their lifeless
Eyes stare
At melanin-filled bodies
With no life left
No fight left
In the dark of the night
In the dark of life in the US of A
How do they recover? Or would they?
Indoctrinated by violence
Socialized by supremacy
Their maturity arrested by the false security of silence
And amnesia
They are traumatized people too

In 2011, I had just finished speaking at a men's event in Dallas, Texas, when an older white man approached me. I assumed he, like the other men I had just spoken to, was going to thank me and share how my message impacted him. Of course, I was also prepared for him to offer criticism as well. His first words to me were, "I'm from West Texas, and I've never heard a Black man speak live in person before." By this, he meant he had never sat under a Black man's teaching or preaching. A little taken aback, I listened intently, not knowing where he was going with this. He continued, "My parents were racist. My grandparents were racist. Racism is all I know. But after hearing you today, I have to tell you that God is doing something in my heart." He then opened up his arms as if to ask me for a hug. We embraced, and he said, "Thank you," and walked away.

In that moment, he was acknowledging that his family socialized him from his childhood to have a racist perspective. He was groomed to be racist. He was taught to hate. He was indoctrinated into believing in the fallacy of his own exalted state robed in whiteness. He was raised to see himself as superior to Black people and to see them as less than. Baptized into intergenerational hate, he never had a chance. While his comments caught me off guard, I was not surprised at all by his confession. I understand that at any given time, I can be in the mall walking alongside, in a coffee shop sitting next to, or actually in conversation at church with a born-and-bred racist.

Some years later, I was preaching at a fairly diverse church, though I consider it culturally white. Another older white man approached me after one of the services had ended. This man approached me in tears. He had a gray beard and gray hair. He was clearly distraught. He began to confess to me, "When I was a kid, I used to see pictures all through my grandfather's house of him standing proudly in front of Black bodies hanging from a tree." My message brought to the surface the memories of his childhood that he likely tried to suppress or had simply forgotten. On this particular Sunday morning, amnesia was disrupted, and the memories began to flood his mind. He began to cry almost uncontrollably with other people waiting patiently to speak to me. What would this man as a young boy do with those images? How does this boy, having grown into an older man, respond to that reality about his grandfather? Now what was I supposed to do with it?

In that moment, almost instinctively, I felt compelled to embrace him. This was not just a broken man; this was a wounded boy wanting to heal. I felt a deep sense of compassion for him. The next thought in my mind was "Be a shepherd to him." I am not claiming responsibility for this man's journey to healing. I did not feel as though I needed to walk with him beyond that moment. But I did sense a divine directive to shepherd him right then. He was a traumatized man who had just been shaken up during a worship service. He apologized to me about what happened to my grandfather and for his own family's participation in the evils of racism toward Black people. I have neither seen nor spoken to him since then. I often wonder how he is carrying the weight of that reality resurfacing. I wonder if he has tried to suppress those memories of a dark family history again. I wonder if he has been wrestling with his own racist tendencies. I'll likely never know.

What disturbed me most of all was the fact that he had likely heard many sermons over the course of his life. In the churches he had visited or been a member of, none had likely ever preached in a way that poked at the open wounds he had. Race, issues surrounding racism, and white supremacy are not deemed important enough to the gospel message to warrant attention even though they are the root causes of racial injustice. The very construction of the idea of race, born from the mind of white supremacists, is an injustice. The religion that claims to have "the answer" to all our problems, both seen and undiscerned, is silent on this issue in most white churches. With this being the case, how many people are sitting in the pews of our churches with unattended trauma in their bodies from their experiences with racism whether they are of the oppressed group or the oppressors?

Traumatized White Bodies

What made this man who my grandfather worked alongside every day decide to execute him on the Sampit River that day in 1953? According to the narrative of events, it was not impulsive, in self-defense, or an accident. It was a planned murder. My grandfather was set up. Two of his coworkers who rode with him on the boat across the river to Goat Island where my grandfather's boss was waiting tried to restrain him. The man who shot him was waiting with a rifle. Shooting my grandfather seemed as natural for him as hunting deer. Witnessing the murder of an African American man, seeing the destruction of another Black body, and resuming life as usual seemed to be as natural as going to church or the grocery store and returning home to be with their families. If it seems natural, then it must be right. But that fallacy is the doorstop to the "open door" that further invites and nurtures white trauma.

Humans were not created to witness, commit, or endure violence without it without it traumatizing their hearts, souls/minds, and bodies. Menakem elaborates on this point: "When a body observes the willful harming of another—especially if it inflicts that harm—it may experience its own *secondary* or *vicarious trauma*. For the past three centuries, many White Americans have experienced this trauma in multiple ways. They controlled, brutalized, and murdered Black bodies. They watched others harm and kill Black bodies. They failed to prevent, stop, or challenge such attacks—or they tried to step in and were brutalized for their attempted interventions."[1] What's interesting is the first person to be traumatized by my grandfather's murder may very well have been the man who shot and killed him. This is not to transfer pity toward him, but it is to highlight the fact that traumatized people traumatize people. He was very well unaware and very likely unwilling to acknowledge the trauma that his whole self experienced that day. It is even less likely that he was aware that he was already carrying trauma in his own body from intergenerational violence.

White people who participate in violence and are indifferent to violence inflicted upon African Americans and other people of color are merely conduits of the violence passed down for centuries. Menakem explains white body trauma:

> In addition, for centuries before that, many Europeans experienced similar trauma as they watched other white bodies be controlled, brutalized, and murdered, or as they were subjected to that oppression themselves by other white bodies. But they were *unable to metabolize the horror* of what they witnessed or experienced, so that horror was stored as trauma in their bodies. This trauma— as well as a variety of self-protective strategies that got built around it—have been passed down and compounded over many generations. They were likely passed down epigenetically as expressions of people's DNA.

They were also passed down as habits, actions . . . beliefs, and ideas. Over generations, the original context was forgotten [not by everyone], and the *trauma became cultural traits or norms.*[2]

African Americans and other people of color have had to navigate white trauma masked by cultural norms. With intergenerational trauma being the deepest layer and violence and racism as the outer layer, in between the two is the layer of white fragility.

White fragility, according to Robin DiAngelo, is a state in which even the smallest amount of racial stress is intolerable, triggering a range of defensive responses as a means of asserting racial control and protection of white advantage.[3] Fragility suggests a level of vulnerability. White vulnerability and white superiority coupled with the fear of Black bodies makes for a perfect storm of factors that produce anti-Black violence. My grandfather, like so many other African Americans during that Jim Crow era, was caught in that perfect storm. But they were not just encountering racism; they were also encountering traumatized white men and women. These white men and women long feared emancipated Black bodies as a threat not only to their safety but also to white supremacy. The natural threat that African American men pose triggers the impulses of a trauma-filled white body intoxicated by the wine of supremacy.

White privilege has a natural tendency to blind the eyes and deafen the ears of the white community to the legitimate social injustices and inequities that African Americans face daily. Privilege plays an important role in the fragility of whiteness. Privilege gives white people the chance to opt out when it comes to coping with, considering, or negotiating with racism at all. It creates the space for white people not having to feel the pain of racial injustice that people of color have no choice but to endure. A reimagined US history from a Black perspective that contains substantial accounts of the dark side of America is optional. Privilege creates a distorted view of reality—a view of reality, particularly about America, that all is well in this great nation and racism is overstated.

This privileged view on reality massages rather than strengthens white people when it comes to engaging issues of race. It does not allow white people to develop intestinal fortitude for uncomfortable conversations on race that center on the actions and inactions of white people. Instead, it causes apathy. Engaging the conversation of racism requires strength of mind/soul, body, and spirit because the whole self—material and immaterial—will feel and carry the weight. This is problematic because the "weight" is typically needed to move a person from apathy to empathy. White privilege weakens not only the ability to think rationally about matters around race and racism but also the ability or even willingness to show compassion.

White Silence

I've come to believe that white silence as a nonresponse to racial bigotry and evidence of racist culture with its pervasive systems and structures is more than just shame, but it is the unconscious fear of addressing their community's trauma. For white people to speak out against racism is to be critical of their own whiteness, since racism, as we know it today, is an invention of white supremacist ideology. White silence actually provides a safe space for racism to continue to flourish uninterrupted. It is as violent as the offense itself.

There was a white woman who witnessed, from a distance, two white men struggling with my grandfather before he was shot who never spoke to law enforcement about it, and if she did, they never followed up with an investigation. A network of cooperating participants on multiple levels holds white silence together. Social power is distributed among the various individuals from eyewitnesses to the medical examiner to police officers. Injustice prevails wherever it finds silence from the community, especially from the white community, because that's where the power lies and where acts of racial injustice will receive permission to continue traumatizing African Americans. Silence, in this case, had implications for both the African American community and the white community. For African Americans, the silence was deafening and led to further solidify their sense of hopelessness. For the white community, the silence was crippling. They were prisoners of their own fears and trauma and continued the cycle of oppressing others rather than become disruptors of oppression.

The prison walls of white silence extend to the holy spaces as well. Many evangelical preachers shy away from preaching, teaching, or informing the congregations about social issues, especially those surrounding race. Imagine carrying a history of trauma in your body as you stand before a congregation who carries the same trauma and are indoctrinated by the same white ideology. It is far safer for one's reputation, health, and church economics to remain silent. Ironically, decades earlier, it was clergy speaking authoritatively from the pulpits who validated slavery and segregation. The difference between the boldness of voices then and the silence now is that white voices were not just the dominant voices but also largely the only voices. Today, "other" voices have whiteness on trial for indictment and it must defend itself.

Whitelash

I was sitting outside my church offices talking on the phone when I noticed an older white man visibly upset as he left the office and passed by me. I asked him if he was all right and if I could help him with anything. With a scowl on his face, he mumbled a few words but got louder when he used profanity. I told him, "Sir, with that attitude, no one is going to help you with whatever you needed." He replied, "Fuck you!" Initially, I was stunned, but I reacted with following him to make sure he left the campus. My rationale was that we had an operating preschool in the building and I wanted this guy off our campus. He continued his verbal assault, challenging me to a fight, and eventually, he said, "I'll come back here and kill you, nigger!" He had no idea that I was going to help him. He had no idea that I had a great-grandfather and a grandfather murdered by white men in the past. He had no idea that in a moment's notice, the trauma and han under the surface of any smile on my face could turn into rage and when unleashed would have crippled him, if not killed him. Yet this white man, while leaving the church campus where I served as a pastor, in his own frustrations for not getting financial help from the church, told me that he would "come back here and kill" me. Why was that his default response? Was his heart filled with hate toward people of color in general or African Americans in particular? The words seem to have formulated effortlessly in his mind, and they came off his lips with the smoothness and precision of a boxer's jab. They carried a historical punch.

If white people do not acknowledge the legacy of their own trauma etched in their genetic memory, they will never heal. Unhealed white bodies will respond accordingly. In the most extreme and the most imperceptible versions of whiteness, they will continue to terrorize people of color. If they never heal, then racism never dies and people of color will always find themselves navigating the landmines of racism—bigotry, microaggressions, and systemic/structural/institutional racism. One reason healing from whiteness is difficult to achieve is because white people generally cannot separate their identity from the label "white." Therefore, they cannot separate themselves from privilege, power, and supremacy. Yet it is the very idea of whiteness as a legally constructed category within the socially constructed ideology of race that has distorted their identity. In addition, it has further marred their image-bearing capacity.

While whiteness in American and global society is synonymous with the norm, the standard, or being whole all on its own, it is far from it. In fact, the invention of whiteness does the opposite. Drawing once again from Willie Jennings's understanding of whiteness as a "deformed building project" as it relates to its implications on world societies, the same is true for what it does to white people's identity. It deforms rather than matures. It takes away from their humanity rather than affirming them being the standard of humanity.

White body trauma is neglected when white people go to great lengths to protect whiteness and all that it represents, beginning with identity. One common tactic is to deflect any responsibility in the ongoing cases of racial injustice. For example, when a professional NFL football player posted on social media that he was chased, treated with excessive force, and wrongfully accused of a crime because he "fit the description," I shared the post on my Facebook page the same day that I read it. A friend of mine, a white conservative evangelical Christian woman, responded on my page that we should "wait for the facts to come out." Her response frustrated me. I asked, "Why is it that white people immediately respond with this statement to a police shooting or misconduct where an African American man or woman dies or is hurt?" I continued, "While you have the luxury of waiting for the facts, can you at least grieve with the mothers, fathers, siblings, and friends of these victims while you wait?" The instinct to religiously deflect accountability for the white police officer, giving him or her the benefit of the doubt while instinctively assigning blame to Black bodies, is incomprehensible. Why was her mind not on the pain that the young man and his family may have been feeling? Why would she, and others, not think first about the mothers who lose their children, the children who lose their parents or siblings, or the husband or wife who loses their spouse?

Menakem says this tactic is a way that "white Americans use white fragility to avoid facing their unhealed trauma."[4] This avoidance invites the preoccupation with assigning blame to Black bodies and protecting other white bodies. It also justifies the higher fatality rate of African Americans when encountering white citizens or law enforcement, since it is assumed we are generally the cause of our own misfortune. If white people do not feel their own trauma enough to grieve and attend to it for the purposes of healing, then they cannot be expected to feel and lament the trauma inflicted upon Black bodies by whiteness in action.

Deformed, immature humanity at the hands of whiteness compulsively responds to the perceived threat of "otherness"—namely, Blackness—with violence. Violence may take the form of attitudes, words, deeds, the white gaze, or even laws and policies. It is instinctual to respond to nonsubjugated Blackness as a threat to whiteness. This is the reason a white person can make a remark or a threat to African Americans and other people of color and then in the next breath declare that they are not racist because they do not hate people of color. Whiteness—not white persons or ethnicity—need not feel anything or be conscious of motivations to act. It functions from a position of insecurity and supremacy. Therefore, otherness is a threat and is naturally inferior. Any challenge or resistance from people of color warrants violence. The essence of whiteness is natural to white people; therefore, the accompanying violence in its various forms in response to Black resistance is natural too.

To illustrate this, I share an encounter with a white man at a megachurch in the Los Angeles area, where I once served as a pastor. A young man was following and harassing his girlfriend in between services. He was yelling profanity and attempting to humiliate her publicly. Several pastors, including me, approached him to try to get him to stop. He paused and surveyed the three of us. The two other pastors, one African American and one Latino, both weighed more than 250 pounds. He turned and stared angrily at me, the smallest of the three. I tried to calm him down, but he took offense. He said to me, "Your skin is darker than mine, and I have a word for people like you." I knew what he meant and where he was headed. I only hoped in that moment that he would not use the forbidden N-word. (I would have likely lost my job as a pastor that day.) Ultimately, he never uttered the word. I took the initiative (certainly a moment where God intervened) and extended love to him in word and in offering an embrace. With tears in his eyes, he received my offer, and we embraced in that moment. That outcome, in my opinion, was the mysterious work of the Holy Spirit.

But we cannot overlook the whiplash-like response of how quickly he resorted to using a racial slur toward me unashamedly. As an African American man, I was either a threat to him or out of line in challenging his privilege to be able to speak how he wanted to his girlfriend. It was instinctual. Soon after the incident, we were taken to the main office, away from the crowd, to talk about what just happened. He apologized profusely and tried to convince me that he was not racist and did not mean to say or insinuate anything racist toward me. But this is what a traumatized white body does; its insecurities and air of supremacy are triggered, and it compulsively reacts with violence of thought, words, gaze, and deeds.

Theological Reflection

Consider the history of the Jewish people as recorded in the Old Testament. They ebbed and flowed in their relationship with YHWH based on their collective willingness to obey. They enjoyed times of peace and prosperity, and because of sin in the forms of injustice within the community and idolatry, they suffered years of hardship at the hands of YHWH and neighboring nations that were at war with them. When examining Israel's history, it can be argued that Israel is a

traumatized nation. They are a nation that has both insti-
gated and received violence from their neighbors.

For four hundred or so years, Israel endured generation
after generation of oppression from slavery. The leadership and favor of Joseph had long been forgotten, and
the people of Israel, foreigners in the land, were vulnerable and exploited as a free labor force. Their time spent
in the Promised Land of Canaan consisted of alternating
seasons of sin and obedience whether they were led by
judges or kings. This back and forth went on until finally
around 597 BC, when Israel began its time in exile from
Jerusalem after being besieged by the Babylonian king
Nebuchadnezzar. It is likely that just witnessing the ruins
of Jerusalem—including the temple, the site of the Divine
presence—was traumatizing.

During the time of Jesus's life and ministry, the Jews were
under Roman occupation. The land was not their own. They
could not move about the region freely and were without a
guarantee of safety. For instance, if a decree was made to kill
all the male Jewish children under two years old, as was done
after the arrival of the boy who would be "King of the Jews,"
there was nothing they could do to prevent it. They were
helpless. The stress from the constant threat of the Romans
had to have been felt daily in their bodies. The leaders of
the Jews would be stuck in between the authority that they
had among the Jewish community and the lack thereof as
it related to the Romans. Undoubtedly, this would have
fostered han—that underlying bitterness and inexpressible
experience of pain—among the Jewish leaders. Experiencing
the daily humiliation of having to submit to Roman rule
while yielding some power among the marginalized had to
have taken its toll.

Jesus, the marginalized among the marginalized, was a rabbi who threatened the authority of the Pharisees and Jewish leaders. He was "otherized" in their minds. He was a poor carpenter from Nazareth, where nothing good was expected to emerge. The Jewish leaders carried the long history of Jewish trauma in their bodies. They clung to their roles and titles as their primary identity markers. There were no alternatives. Who are they without those titles and roles in the Jewish community? Who were they without the authority and supremacy among the Jewish people? Traumatized bodies ask these questions. They instantly assess the threat level and respond instinctively according to the level of the threat. The more compliant people are, the less of a threat they pose. The more resistant or uncontrollable they are, the greater the threat they are. These were "holy" men with violent impulses. The tendency to condemn, to place law and ritual over human dignity, or to execute an innocent man who embodied an existential threat to their roles as Jewish leaders were all manifestations of violent impulses.

Power and unattended trauma in the same body is dangerous. Anyone identified as an "other" is at risk of violence and oppression. It can be argued that one factor, aside from God's will, that contributed directly to the execution of Jesus Christ is the unattended Jewish trauma contained in the bodies of the Jewish leaders. The "otherness" of Jesus was socioeconomic and theological. Both challenged the social and intellectual elites and the pious. Traumatized Jewish bodies under the tyranny of their own theological authority and social power, inherent to their identity, were self-destructive and destructive to the community. Likewise, whiteness, power, and being the standard of humanity are self-traumatizing and traumatizing to the entire community.

Reflection Questions

Are you aware of any trauma you may carry in your body?

Do you think there are attitudes and actions you show that are born from trauma and have an adverse effect on others?

What methods of healing trauma have you engaged in? What methods are you familiar with that you recommend?

PART 3

Reaching
Redemption

CHAPTER 8

Intergenerational Healing

Let us create shared space
If you bring the sacredness of the past
Will you trust me to interpret your wisdom for your
    children?
I am your child
The fruit of your pioneering labor
I've been inspired by your resilience
I am not conceived without it
Which means I am sacred too
Will you trust me to impart wisdom back to you?
That way we heal each other's wounds

My grandmother learned how to gird herself in both healthy and unhealthy ways. She used whatever resources were available to her over the course of her life. Her body's constriction at the retriggering of the trauma it carried became a natural disposition in her face, her hands, and her gait. There was no such thing as therapy in our community back when she grew up. We had made little progress in that regard even in the days of my youth. "Keep on keepin' on" was the therapy. You just tucked away your sorrows and frustrations and kept moving forward, trusting that better days would come. We, as a people, seem to be perpetually traveling in the wilderness hoping to reach Canaan, where there would be neither injustice nor inequity motivated by the skin color and physical attributes of our African ancestry. I recall longing for the day that I could see her breathe easy. I wanted to see her body not in its tightened posture. I would not get a glimpse of that until the last few months of her life when she came to visit me in Los Angeles.

I believe in the power of prayer. I only wish I had the maturity, wisdom, and understanding to have prayed more frequently and passionately when I was young. In the last few months of her life, my grandmother had visited California to spend some time resting and relaxing at the home of her brother Mickey in Fontana. She had just lost her son—Bobby—who passed away about seven months earlier. She was his caretaker for much of the time he was ill. She was visibly tired. When she came out, I picked her up and brought her to my home so the two of us could spend a day together. She rode in the passenger seat with that constricted posture that had become all too familiar. That night when we arrived at my home and she prepared for bed, I could tell she was still carrying the stress of the death of her son. She said she had not been able to sleep well for years. She could not remember the last time she had a solid night's sleep. I said to her without hesitation, "Grandma, let me pray for you." She allowed me to lay hands on her and pray. I continued to pray for her as she slept until I fell asleep. The next morning, I asked her how she slept. She looked at me, cracked a smile, and said, "I had the best sleep I've had in years." She was eating from the fruit of her years of prayers over me and her diligence in "making" me go to church every Sunday. This was beneficial for her, but it was also a gift for me.

Here I was returning the favor to my grandmother by praying over her in her time of vulnerability. Years ago the roles would have been reversed. She had sown the seeds of faith all those years, and it was finally shown that those seeds landed on "good" soil. I was reciprocating back to my grandmother what she had done for me for many years. In some ways, I was shepherding her. As I reflect on the moment, it was healing for both of us. It was a tangible form of God's grace.

I could never explain why when I would watch a television show or a movie with any scene that involved transracial mentorship or expressions of love, solidarity, or reconciliation I would get emotional. I never understood where that came from. Whether it was an older white man mentoring a younger Black man or young boy or an older Black woman doing the same with a young white girl, the same emotions would surface, even if it were a commercial. Where did this come from? It was certainly nothing I had planned on or thought about. It was not anything I had consciously desired.

Meanwhile, if the very next scene in the movie or television show was depicting any type of racist behavior toward people of color, I could feel the intensity of indignation consume my body. I have lived in that tension all my life. I have functioned in the space between a desire to see reconciled relationships, especially between Black and white, and the anger that arises when I witness the evil of racist ideologies, attitudes, and actions.

I am the embodiment of redemptive prayer. When my father told me about his prayer over me while I was in my mother's womb, it all began to make sense. This was God's grace all along. I believe this was something God had deposited in me in response to a young man's desperate prayers over his unborn son. My father's prayers—and I am sure my mother's and my grandparents' prayers as well—would be answered. My life is the fruit of those prayers. The fact that I do not carry the same degree of rage and hate that my father carried is a testament to the power of prayer. One could also argue that, practically speaking, the fact that I am a generation removed from my grandfather's murder played an insulating role in preserving my heart in ways that proximity did not afford my father. I would counter with the fact that God works even in those practical, providential ways to bring healing and restoration to our lives.

Prayer is significant for our collective healing. It must be foundational for our ethics moving toward progress. We can take all the practical steps that may be presented in this book or elsewhere, but those methods must be rooted in prayer.

No More Secrets

I am often asked if the making of *Open Wounds* (2019) has brought any closure or healing to our family. I would say it has. It has brought a degree of healing for my father, myself, and our relationship in particular. My father finally has the opportunity to speak about the father he never knew. The film has provided a therapeutic space for him to reflect in interviews with his son as he both shares and learns about his father. It has been a space for tears, for laughter, for sharing the disappointment, and for honest confessions about the implications of my grandfather's death on my father's life. Everything about the event was kept a secret. He never knew about his father until he was in his late thirties. Now there are fewer secrets. Light is being shed. The nature of (sun)light is to provide life-giving energy. This is what telling our story and engaging my father in reflection about his father has done for us; it has provided life. It has been a pathway for a stronger reconciled relationship between the two of us.

The secrets of our families and communities delay our healing. Sometimes an X-ray cannot find the cause of a health concern beyond what the bone structure reveals. Ligament and cartilage damage are hidden from the doctors—ambiguous at best. When the X-ray is insufficient, the doctor may order an MRI or a CT scan. Those tests normally are able to reveal or clarify what the X-ray could not identify at all or could not identify with full clarity. The conversations I have had with my father, my grandparents before they passed away, and their siblings have been the MRIs and CT scans that reveal the depth and nature of the trauma our family has endured. They educate me as to what intergenerational trauma/issues/curses I have felt in my own body. They help me identify sources of my own inner conflicts and inclinations.

Healing is often a painful task. It was not easy for my father or my uncles to enact the concept of *Sankofa*—"to go back and get"—and to relive the memories of the tragedies and the people they miss dearly. While this is no easy task, it is more self-destructive to simply store the secrets of the past and believe they will go away. Rather, these realities gnaw at the soul of a person. Keeping secrets is as effective as trying to use Band-Aids to cover up a deep cut that actually needs stitches. The cut still risks infection even though it is covered to the public. It requires much deeper cleansing.

We can learn much more from the Samaritan man in the story Jesus tells in Luke 10. A man was beaten and left for dead. Obviously, he is scarred with open cuts and bruises.

We know this because the Samaritan man used wine and oil to disinfect and soothe what were likely "open wounds." He gets to his knees; he uses his own resources to pour upon the wounds. He bandages them up. Then he helps the man to his animal in order to get him to a place to rest and recover. The Samaritan man represents the younger, less-traumatized generation. The man left for dead is the older generation of African Americans whose bodies have gone before ours and have taken heavier, more consistent social blows than we have. These intergenerational conversations where we give space to speak of the horrors of the past while we learn from them are our way of tending to the wounds. The prayers that pass between the two generations are the balm of the wine and oil that facilitate healing.

Painful healing when it comes to the topic of racism is not just a prescription for African Americans and people of color. It is for white people as well. I preached at the Black History Month chapel service at a high school in the Los Angeles area. This was a very wealthy private school that was predominantly white. I shared the story of my grandfather, but I also shared the collective history of African Americans from the tragedies to the inventions. After chapel, many of the kids came forward to shake my hand and thank me for the message. One young man in particular came to me with a heavy heart. When I asked what the problem was, he shared that he had recently found out that his family once owned slaves in the South. Prior to learning this, he had no idea that his family participated in one of the darkest times—if not *the* darkest time—in American history. You could see the weight of that reality in his body. He was a tall kid, about 6′3″, but in that moment, the knowledge of his family's history stole inches from his height.

He reminded me of my grandmother's body constricting and getting smaller when I asked her about the tragedy in our family's history. Maybe the constricting of the body and the shortening of the spine are necessary responses before the exhaling and freedom of healing.

Giving Voice—Counsel of Elders and Youth

In 2009, I visited the Auschwitz concentration camp in Poland. From the time we entered the camp, it felt like the processional and recessional parts of a long funeral. It was a visit that stirred up a level of grief that I had not experienced in many years. We navigated the grounds in and out of buildings with images and artifacts that transport visitors back to a dark time. I could see the people. Literally, I saw pictures of those men, women, and children who were incarcerated. I saw the remains of shaved hair, suitcases, glasses, and baby shoes behind glass windows that made the holocaust even more real. Even as I reflect while writing these words, I can feel the same visceral response in my body that I had in that moment. My body feels the tension from my head to my feet, as it felt when I stood at the location where Jews were executed by firing squad. The moment, the location, and the recollection of the events were surreal.

We approached one of the barracks where the Jews were imprisoned. Just before entering one of them, there was a sign just outside that said, "He who forgets the past is condemned to repeat it." This is a famous quote by George Santayana. It is a reminder that amnesia may cause us to retrace steps that lead us back to a destructive past. Memory not only allows us to appreciate past events; it offers an opportunity to learn or relearn lessons from the past as well *(Sankofa)*. It is the counsel of the elders telling their stories and educating generations to follow. It is imperative that we heed their voices through stories, film, art, and the artifacts left for us. In some ways, memory triggers and retraumatizes, but in some ways, it can heal wounds.

Just like my father now has the opportunity to exhale by talking about his father and seeing the truth told through his son through the medium of film, so it is with the Jews who see their stories being told for millions to understand the suffering that has so shaped their lives. Although Auschwitz is a symbol of pain—physical, emotional, psychological, and fatal wounds—it also stands as a monument of resiliency. To know this side of the truth of the Holocaust is healing for a wounded community.

To know the reality of slavery is painful, but it also speaks of the strength of my ancestors to endure. To understand the Jim Crow–era ethos that included lynching Black bodies at an unimaginable rate is traumatic, but it also reveals the collective inner fortitude of my predecessors. To recall the events surrounding the lynching of my grandfather is a grueling journey, but it also connects dots and makes sense of how individuals in my family and the family as a whole have been formed. This then helps me understand my own formation. My people chose none of these realities. We have nothing to be ashamed of. They were imposed upon us. Carrying the shame of our past is toxic. Telling the truth of our past so that the following generations would know the substance from which they came is a healing balm.

We must hear the voices of our youth as well. Paul writes, encouraging Timothy, to "let no one despise [his] youth" (1 Timothy 4:12 ESV). That same exhortation has a place today for young minds with great passion and energy. While age may indicate less experience, it does not necessarily equate to less wisdom, especially when their lives reflect such wisdom and maturity. Intergenerational healing requires the voices of our elders telling their stories, educating us, mentoring us, and reminding us of the good, bad, and ugly of our past. It also requires our elders to listen to the voices of those who have followed their footsteps. The elders must be willing and able to appreciate the fruit of their labor. The youth, relatively speaking, is their fruit. We see history and present times from a different perspective: one that is not detached from theirs but shaped and influenced by theirs. We want to remember the labor and pioneering of the past with the innovation and creativity of the present. In the tradition passed on to us as far back as the land of our ancestors, we want to honor them.

From our vantage point, we tell the stories back to them. First, this indicates that we've been listening. We heard them. Their work and their words were not in vain. Second, we are able to identify the ways trauma has manifested itself in their lives and projected onto ours. When a person is in the fight, they do not always know why and how they got injured. They just know they are hurting. Someone on the outside of that particular fight may be able to view the "footage" of history, play Monday morning quarterback, and share how deep that injury might be. They may understand the depths in a way that the injured does not simply because the one who is injured had to feel the brunt of the injury passed down to them.

In recent years, I finally got the chance to have conversations with my father where I could discuss the ways in which his pain impacted my life. At first, there was denial and deflecting full responsibility, but he honored me by hearing me out. I shared this with the intent not to condemn but rather to bring clarity and even confess the unforgiveness I stored in my heart because of his unrepentant behavior over the years. I honored him in return by giving him the space to share where he was emotionally and mentally during my youth. In real time, he was trying to make sense of his actions. We have laughed together, cried together, and sat in silent awkwardness as well. At some point in this journey, my father (the elder) told me (the youth) that he considered me one of the mentoring voices in his life as he embarked on a journey of healing. This would not have happened if I was not willing to listen to him and if he was not willing to hear me out. The catalyst for these healing conversations was the horror of his father's murder.

This is also the case for the white community. What is common between people of color—particularly African Americans—and white families is the painful past that must be discussed and the wounds from that past that must be attended to. Typically, older white people want to move on from the past. It is likely because they are closer to the guilt from the reality of the horrors inflicted upon African Americans. They may know people who lynched, who fought for segregation, or who hated the "otherness" of African Americans. They themselves may actually be those people. Younger white people are not as familiar with the history of racism, at least not in grasping the degree of its barbarity. However, when their eyes are opened, they have the potential to be fiercely zealous in speaking out against it even to their own family members.

In 2019, I taught a class at Ozark Christian College in Joplin, Missouri, entitled "A New Race: Reimagining Biblical Ethics toward Racial Solidarity." It was my first time teaching this class, and I was excited and nervous at the same time. I was excited because I had the opportunity to teach from the research I had done over the previous two years while working on my master's degree at Fuller Theological Seminary. I was nervous because I knew only white students, given the demographics of the school and the area of the country it was located, would likely attend the class. This was confirmed when I received the short list of six students who signed up for the course. I wanted to teach with honesty and authenticity, but I wanted to be sure to maintain my pastoral voice. I did not design the class to "stick it" to white people. I wanted to educate them.

My approach to this course was to begin with a genealogical method. After introducing myself and having them do the same, with each of us telling something about ourselves, I took them back to the trans-Atlantic slave trade. For the sake of time, I gave them a survey of the history of race relations in the United States. I worked my way from the massacre and annihilation of Native people to the first slaves to reach American soil in 1619, to the Trail of Tears, through slavery and Jim Crow, to Japanese incarceration camps, to the civil rights movement, and landed on the current Black Lives Matter era. As I navigated history on my PowerPoint presentation, my eyes navigated the room to get a feel for how they were receiving the information. After an hour or so, we took a break. Once we returned, I needed to check the pulse of the class.

One young lady sitting in the front row had a blank stare with a bit of a scowl on her face. I paused and then asked her if she wanted to share so that we could process together. She simply said, "I'm angry." I followed up, asking her, "Why are you angry?" She said, "Because my parents never taught me this stuff. No one ever told me this before." I felt for her. This was not a surprise. Most young white Americans know very little about the history of racism in the United States. Their knowledge is superficial and myopic at best. She indicated that she knew she needed to have a conversation with them because she had questions. This conversation she knew needed to happen will not be easy, but it is necessary. I suspect they will have a perspective of history that is insufficient for her. I anticipate her fresh eyes on history will offer an alternative interpretation of the effects of such a past. Her body likely responded to the images and the statistics in ways that are different from her parents and grandparents, who were formed by a different ideology within a different ethos. Their world was different from the one she lives in today.

In that same class, a young white woman shared a story that I believe is relevant for my point in this chapter of intergenerational conversations and engagement to bring forth healing. She told the story of an experience in high school when she was dating an African American schoolmate. When her grandfather found out, he was adamant that she not "date a Black guy and bring him into this family." Her revelation to her family and her grandfather's response obviously created tension among them, particularly between her and her grandfather. Her mother intervened and confronted her grandfather. Being that he was a professed Christian, she spoke in his language. Her mother told him he was in sin because he was acting as a racist by disliking this young man simply because he is Black. A day or so went by, and apparently her grandfather could not shake those words. He was convicted to the point that he apologized to the family and confessed that his daughter was correct; he was a racist. He then had her invite the young man to his home for dinner. When the young man arrived, her grandfather hugged him and kissed him on the cheek to show an outward sign that he was truly remorseful for his attitude and actions. The young lady's mother partnered with her and participated in the role of the youth speaking back to the elder. He did not look down upon their youth. He listened. He repented. He exhibited actions that confirmed repentance that he otherwise would not have ever shown.

My film *Open Wounds* (2019) has functioned to foster intergenerational healing. It has functioned to provide a space for transracial and intergenerational dialogue. There have been young people—Black, white, Asian, Latino/Latina, and others—who have expressed gratitude for educating them on the reality of the legacy of past racial tragedies and their lasting effects today. There have also been older generations of African Americans grateful for the telling of a story that had been replicated in many families across this nation. Older white people have expressed gratitude for telling the story and giving them a perspective they had not considered—intergenerational trauma. They have also grieved at this reality (although some still walk away not understanding racism beyond explicit acts of bigotry while neglecting the systemic/structural racism that the film aimed to depict).

There must be transracial intergenerational communal space that is the context for healing. This is the table. As I said before, this table must be set by people of color inviting the white community to be there. It is a role of discipleship that white people must be willing to enter into. They should come with a humble attitude and a learning posture. But among people of color, especially African Americans, there must be shared authority among the young and the older generations. Healing is somewhere in the midst of that engagement.

Above all, when the dialog has ended, there still needs to be justice. The prayers and conversations are a necessary start, but justice is healing. Prayer is spiritual engagement, but justice is social engagement. Prayer is mindful of wrongs that have been done and could potentially be exacted upon people while invoking God for intervention. The work of justice is active participation with the very God that is called upon to make wrongs right. If there is such a thing as intergenerational trauma, then there can also be such a thing as intergenerational healing. This healing involves prayer, dialog, and justice.

As a man of faith, I believe justice may come in two ways: poetic justice (instances when God supernaturally intervenes) and the work of justice, when we participate with God in doing the work of justice as God expects of us (Micah 6:8; Matthew 23:23). My uncle Nate told me the story that when he was older and in college and still felt the desire to take some form of revenge on the man who killed his father, his grandmother Hattie Robinson told him, "Don't do anything, God'll touch 'em." He took that to mean that God will get justice in God's time as God sees fit. When my uncle came home from visiting from college he found out that one son of his father's murderer was killed in a water skiing accident when he had lost control and fell into a water moccasin pit in the same area along the same island where my grandfather was killed. This was so dramatic that it was hard for me to believe. Not long after that another son was killed in a boating accident on the same river. There is no other way for me to describe these events than *poetic justice*. While no one cheers for their deaths, one cannot help but to feel a sense of peace that there was a force (God) that intervened to get justice—in such dramatic fashion—when the white power structure denied my family that opportunity.

We can also engage in the *work of justice* to bring healing. The work is hard, draining, and even risky, but simultaneously empowering to those whose voices would now be heard and whose bodies would now be seen. When there is some form of change—arrest and guilt, change of laws, awareness of injustice, etc.—one may feel a sense of vindication that something good was done and emerged out of much tragedy, trauma, and pain.

I felt a sense of healing and empowerment when I saw the youth of our city organize and lead a march in response to George Floyd's murder. I was tired. They had renewed energy. It was important that I come to the table they set to show my support as they stood and marched for solidarity as ones taking the baton from their predecessors. I imagine it was equally important for them to see my generation marching with them. They were speaking back to us. They were reassuring us that the work would continue: the work of justice and ultimately of healing.

Theological Reflection

Generally, when we think about the concept of the table, we think about sharing. At the table—whether biblically or traditionally—in many families, we share food, laughter, tears, and we share opinions and feelings in order to resolve conflict. It truly is sacred space. Jesus shared his final meal at the table with his disciples. They shared the meal while Jesus shared prophetic revelation. There was also a bit of conflict with Judas present before he left to go and betray Jesus. One would say Judas violated sacred space. More importantly, the table, as a fixture in most homes, provides an opportunity for dialogue that leads to empowerment and healing between parties sharing the space. But it is critical who we invite to the table. We must be willing to invite perspectives and experiences that sharpen ours, not just those already in agreement with what we believe.

This transracial and intergenerational space is vital to the community. It is not just about "getting along" or simply showing unity. It is about coming to the space to do necessary work toward healing and righting wrongs. Imagine a family coming together after a disruptive conflict or maybe after a traumatic event in the community (e.g., 9/11) to have a meal. Parents and children alike come to the table to break bread and share their hearts, clear the air, cry, or ask questions as they process the events. At the table, all are heard. Everyone's voice and perspective are valued.

God affirms all persons in the range of seasons of life represented by the family. Healing is a collaborative affair in God's economy. Proverbs is filled with axioms of wisdom in general, but it is explicit when it comes to youth heeding the wisdom of elders. For elders, wisdom is born from a wealth of life experiences. They have a duty to share it with the youth.

Proverbs 1:8–9 says, "Hear, my child, your father's instruction, and do not reject your mother's teaching; for they are a fair garland for your head, and pendants for your neck." Proverbs 3:1–2 continues, "My child, do not forget my teaching, but let your heart keep my commandments; for length of days and years of life and abundant welfare they will give you." Though they have the freedom to reject wisdom, it would behoove them to receive instructions and lessons from elders, as they contain wisdom with life-giving potential. Wisdom passed down in the form of history and storytelling is not only fruitful for education but also affirming and empowering for youth with the capacity to positively influence the trajectory of the next generation.

What is this concept of wisdom that is being ex[...] at the "table"? Tracking its etymology, wisdom is made [...] of two words that when put together mean the quality of being wise or "knowing." The first half of this old English word (wise) means "having the power to discern rightly."[1] The second half of the word (-dom) means the state or quality of.[2] Simply put, wisdom can be understood to mean the quality and power of discerning right from wrong.

Like the elders that impart wisdom to the youth of the family, the converse is also true that there is wisdom that can be given that comes upstream from youth to elders. Biblically, wisdom is more than just "discerning rightly." It has more to do with the practice of that discernment: the application of the knowledge that one has received. In Psalm 119:99–100, the psalmist declares, "I have more understanding than all my teachers, for your decrees are my meditation. I understand more than the aged, for I *keep* your precepts" (emphasis mine). The psalmist claims to observe God's words. What is being conveyed here is that the psalmist obeys, by putting into action, God's word. By applying God's word, the psalmist, who the text suggests is a youth relative to the elders, is as knowledgeable or as wise as the elders.

This idea of keeping God's precepts or God's word is found in Pauline biblical literature. Paul exhorts Timothy not to let anyone belittle him because of his youth "but set the believers an example in speech and conduct, in love, in faith, in purity" (1 Timothy 4:12). This is Paul's charge for Timothy to not only *know* but *keep* and practice what he was taught. The wisdom of the youth is embodied and made concrete in these ways: their passion, their courage, and their willingness to sacrifice their bodies for the ideals of the greater good.

atively and literally, is a sacred space
wisdom in order to respond as a family/
.ie challenges and issues of the day. It is
: the wisdom of the elders is honored and the
___ ...sdom of the youth is welcomed. That exchange
should be mutually empowering and should foster healing in the wake of conflict or catastrophe. How does that
relate to healing the trauma passed down to young African
Americans from racial injustice? The wisdom that is handed
down empowers the next generation to identify and undo
the disorienting nature of racism—and more specifically,
white supremacy—as it relates to the destruction of one's
humanity. It aids the next generation in discerning what is
the appropriate "ought" in terms of an ethical response to
undermine its systematic and oppressive manifestations. The
wisdom applied and spoken back to the elders from the youth
assures the elders that their pioneering work was not in vain.

Reflection Questions

Do you feel as though you have a "table" to sit at and
engage in healing dialogue with those of a generation
older or younger than yours?

If you are young, what wisdom do you think would
be beneficial for you to share with elders? If you are
older, what wisdom do you think is beneficial to share
with the youth?

Would you be eager to sit at a "table" with those of
another generation and another race, or would you
be intimidated by that idea?

CHAPTER 9

Racial Solidarity

The table and the cross are inextricably tied
The King came
He ate
And he died
He resurrected so that death's victory is denied
But first
He became like me
He suffered like me
He grieved with me
He was oppressed as if he were me
He too was an "other"
He too was pushed to the margins
He understood
He knew the view from the feeding trough
From Egypt
From Calvary
From the other side of the tracks
I'm grateful for the solidarity Immanuel

When I began to share the story of my grandfather's murder, many well-meaning white people would say, "I'm so sorry about what happened to your grandfather." Some would even go as far as saying,

ing to get justice." I sincerely appreci-
once shared with my uncle that people,
people, are honoring his father every time
. His response, though initially shocking,
...... me more than I imagined. He said, with
a tinge of bitterness, "They should have honored him in
1953 when they killed him. They should have spoken up
back then." Of course, he was not speaking of these people
responding to my story today as those who should have
spoken up back then, but he was speaking of white people in
general. "They" should have said something. "They" should
have wanted to make it right. Wouldn't any decent human
being? I appreciated his raw honesty. Actually, I expected
nothing less from him. He was right. An apology today is
insufficient. The wound is still there and unattended to. Does
that mean only justice matters at this point?

Empathetic white people today usually apologize for what
happened in the past, or in an attempt to encourage me, they
remind me of many truths that I am already certain of. I've
come to a point in my life and journey in my faith where I
am in no need of the reminder that I am equal to anyone
else. I do not need anyone to tell me that I too am a child of
God and that God loves me. I am already confident in these
things. I do not need anyone to reassure me that racism is
wrong and needs to be eradicated. I am fully aware of the
reprehensibility of this human/social construction. I try to
feel the sincerity of their apologies, but it does not change
the fact that there was a culture of white supremacy that
legally annihilated my grandfather and many other African
Americans during his day and still has breathing power today.

What killed my grandfather and prevented justice to
takes its course was not just one white man with a gun and

two white men trying to hold my grandfather down. It was a culture that believed white was superior and was the standard by which all humanity is measured. It was the structures that had been in place for hundreds of years that have matured and evolved to protect whiteness at the destruction of Black selves in more creative ways. What killed my grandfather was an entire network that he was born into—one that executed and justified his death.

Those structures still exist today. Black bodies are still destroyed at rates higher than any other group. Black bodies are formed and shaped by social structures to increase the likelihood of imprisonment. In fact, nearly 50 percent of exonerations are African Americans who have been falsely accused and imprisoned.[1] The criminal justice system ensures that Black bodies continue to be void of inherent dignity.

This is why an apology is not enough. An apology does not address the systemic/structural issues that persist today. An apology only shows empathy for events that occurred in the past or occur in the present but has little relevance for the systems that operate oftentimes imperceptibly in history and today. Until apologies can translate into action that leads to policy changes and cultural ethos, it is merely the beginning. The acknowledgment is just a start.

"Dance with Me"

Once again, I was preaching in front of a multiethnic but culturally homogeneous white church community in the Los Angeles area. I shared an illustration of dancing as an analogy for the work we must do for racial justice. I described the intimacy of dancing, the connectedness of two bodies moving in sync one moment and in beautiful contrast the next. Dancing is not just fun and entertaining; there is vulnerability in dancing because both partners must be interdependent with each other in order to be successful. The close proximity allows for seeing and feeling each other's flaws and weaknesses while still appreciating each other's strengths. There is also risk involved. The risk is that you may be exposed as the one without rhythm or someone who is not in tune with his or her body or the body of the dance partner. If this is the case, you disrupt the rhythm of your dance partner.

At the end of the illustration, I mentioned that I needed someone or some people to dance with me. By this, I meant I needed people who were not afraid to come close enough to my context as an African American man who has a unique history in America. I represent a people who share that history. I needed people to not be afraid to shorten the distance between me and them, between my community and theirs. It is in this intimacy that white people can understand the existential reality of African Americans beyond the white lens. In this "dance," they show that they are *with* us, willing to acknowledge and remove the unconscious "otherness" so that there is authentic brotherhood and sisterhood.

In response to my illustration and request, an older white woman approached me after the service and simply said, "I'll dance with you." She said it with tears nearly falling from her eyes. She got it. She understood what I was asking of her and what she was willing to commit to. I do not know if she would follow through with her statement. I suspect that is not for me to know. However, she is claiming in her statement that she is willing to take risks, to immerse herself in my context to learn and feel and to appreciate my strengths and weaknesses while exposing her own.

In my documentary short film, *Open Wounds* (2019), a friend of mine named Bobby Harrison has become a "dance partner" with people of color. Bobby is a white pastor in the Pasadena, California, area and a classmate of mine at Fuller Theological Seminary. Bobby described an evening when he and a friend got the news of a vigil that clergy in Pasadena had organized for prayer, song, and reflection in response to a shooting of another unarmed African American man. The vigil, he says, turned into a protest, and suddenly they found themselves in the midst of a Black Lives Matter march. He recalls looking over to his friend and asking, "Is this a Black Lives Matter march? Because we didn't sign up for this." His intentions were to show up, pray, "sing kum ba yah," and go home. He shared that upon reflection, they needed to feel in their bodies, in their feet, what it meant to respond to the racial injustice that African Americans have had to respond to for centuries. He returned home, and just like that, he could be home on another part of the city, close his front door, kiss his daughter, and sit next to his wife and leave the other part of the city where African Americans gather with lament, frustration, and rage.

What Bobby described in the film was the solidarity that is required to be a part of substantive change. He showed up to a vigil, and before he knew it, he was doing a dance of lament with the Black community. His body needed to be in close proximity, in fact, immersed in the emotions—from pain to anger—of the community. He was willing to take on the vulnerability of the Black community as his own. Bobby and his friend embodied the dance in the sense that their bodies were both moving in sync with Black and

Brown bodies and a beautiful aesthetic contrast, adding to the mosaic of humanity pieced together to create one picture. Bobby embodied the humility that suggests he is here to be a part of something, not to fix or take over with his privilege as a white man. He laid down his privilege, and in his vulnerability, he was able to "be with" in a way that those marching and protesting needed him to be.

"Showing up" was an act of solidarity. You cannot dance without showing up. You cannot dance without your body being present, without your eyes and hands and feet involved. The work of racial solidarity and racial justice requires embodiment, not just conversation and exchange of ideas from safe distances. There must be risk, and something may have to die. Whatever causes many white people to cling to self-preservation or even white supremacy in response to the mere conversation around racial injustice must die. Baptism's like this must occur. This baptism or cultural immersion—death, burial and resurrection to new vision, engagement, and passion—for justice is necessary. This is especially true for white Christians who claim that we are all brothers and sisters in Christ. They claim to be witnesses for the love of Christ. Usually this witness takes the form of compassion in feeding the poor, building homes in Mexico or wells in Africa, or sending money to sponsor a child in poverty in another country. Rarely do we see white evangelical Christians take a vocal or physical stand of solidarity with people of color against racism. The silence and absence of white Christians are un-Christlike. You cannot separate our witness from the cross and its meaning.

What Would Jesus Do? (Theological Reflection)

"What would Jesus do?" is one of the most famous rhetorical questions ever asked. The answer to that question begins at the cross. But I want to go back to the beginning of Jesus's life in the flesh to show that his life was marked by solidarity with humanity. It is largely understood that Isaiah prophesied that the Messiah's name would be Immanuel, "God with us."[2] This is the essence of Jesus's life whether it is to confront injustice, to comfort the downtrodden, or to feed the hungry. When properly understood and embodied, the gospel message is the "dance."

According to the New Testament, God begins a physical manifestation of solidarity by taking on the form of a human.[3] "God could have decided to stand with humanity in the mystery and invisibility of the Spirit, but chose to immerse God's self in the human experience as one of us."[4] Jesus—as the revelation of God, God incarnate—begins his life from the margins. The Magi meet him with gifts for worship as he lay in a feeding trough in Bethlehem (the House of Bread). Not only does God show solidarity with humanity, but God also appears in the form of and in the midst of the most vulnerable. God did not show up in a palace sequestered from the people.

God did not come in the type of power that humans would expect for the Creator of the universe to appear. God's power confounds us. There is power in the vulnerability and humility that marks the person and life of Jesus. Jesus did not impose himself onto others, but he presented himself to the "least of these," the marginalized, the oppressed, and the vulnerable. This is the model. This is the work to combat racial injustice. Jesus's life and ministry was a dance with those thousands who needed food to eat, the lepers who desired to be healed, and the demonized man who received deliverance.

This dance concluded with a medley, or "mixtape" remix, of songs from a final meal in fellowship with his disciples to being arrested, beaten, crucified, executed, and buried. The final act of his life was a sacrificial and solidaric act of love on behalf of others. I use the term *other* because God is completely otherworldly compared to humans. The solidarity of Jesus—the God-man—meant freedom for humanity. It revealed God's intentions for the destruction of every form of sin from individual acts to laws and policies that undergird social/structural sin. Without this act of solidarity with humanity and especially the poor, the captives, the blind, and the oppressed,[5] humanity does not experience the *zoe*—abundant life—Jesus offers.

Many white evangelical Christians are advocates for the idea of racial reconciliation but are uncomfortable with racial solidarity. I once met with a teacher at the high school that invited me to speak at their Black History Month chapel service. We discussed my potential role in assisting in the school's efforts toward diversity and inclusion. I'm not a fan of "diversity" as a goal for an organization. The simple act of admitting and arranging bodies within the organization can accomplish the cosmetics of diversity but never address systemic/structural/institutional racism. She spoke to me about racial reconciliation being a primary theme of their efforts. I responded by offering another perspective and goal. I told her my focus is on racial solidarity rather than reconciliation. She asked to hear more about my choice of "solidarity" over "reconciliation"; she admitted it made her uncomfortable and that others would be likely to feel the same. I was surprised, given the fact that solidarity preceding reconciliation was the way of Jesus.

The words in the New Testament translated as reconciliation or reconciled are most often referred to in the context of Ephesians 2 and 2 Corinthians 5. It is true that reconciling humanity (and, in fact, creation) is the end result of Jesus's work on the cross as the sacrificial Lamb for all of humanity. Ephesians 2:14,16 (ESV) says, "He himself is our peace . . . and might reconcile us both to God in one body *through the cross*" (emphasis mine). In other words, reconciliation through Christ is the fruit of the sacrificial and solidaric work of Christ on the cross. What Paul writes in 2 Corinthians 5:18,19 reinforces this idea: "All this is from God, who reconciled us to himself through Christ, and has given us the ministry of reconciliation; that is, in Christ God was reconciling the world to himself." Once again, "through Christ" and "in Christ" point to the solidarity that God showed with the human experience by taking on flesh and to the solidarity that God showed in saving/healing humanity by taking on the cross.

Solidarity cannot be taken for granted. The cultural romanticism with reconciliation endangers the necessary work of solidarity required to combat white supremacy. Reconciliation today, without emphasis on the solidaric work of Jesus that makes reconciliation possible, has been diluted into a mandate for African Americans to forgive white people, extend grace to white people, and love them. The onus is placed on Black people to do the work of solidarity, as white people only need to apologize or admit that racism exists and it is wrong. Today, it only requires that they are willing to post #BlackLivesMatter on their social media platforms. This is still a white supremacist ethic. This approach still centers white bodies, perspectives, and feelings.

Jesus did the opposite. Jesus centered the marginalized, the oppressed, the poor—all those considered the "least of these" in society. Jesus relinquished his privilege of being God in flesh and kept the onus upon himself to "do the work." This does not mean it will be an easy task. This does not suggest the work comes without internal and external struggle. In fact, Jesus agonized in the garden of Gethsemane before authorities arrested him. He prayed that the Father would "remove this cup" from him.[6] Yet he would find himself on the cross fully committed to performing the solidaric act that would reconcile humanity and creation back to the Father. It is this ministry that we inherited as Christians. We cannot simply reframe the cross, sanitizing it to be something that is pleasant to take upon ourselves. We must see the blood-soaked timber. It is imperative that we notice the holes left by the nails driven through the flesh of Jesus. We also cannot afford to ignore the trauma experienced by his mother who watched in horror.

We Can't Breathe

After the public lynching of George Floyd on Memorial Day of 2020, there was a show of solidarity in the protests across the country and globe. The protests consisted no longer of just African Americans but of every ethnic background imaginable. The anger was felt by everyone regardless of race. Much like Harrison, people felt it in their feet. Although there is still much practical work that needs to be done, Black people generally were pleased and relieved to see the show of solidarity and support—particularly from white people. It seemed as though they finally believed us.

There was no protest for my grandfather. There was no show of solidarity, only silence. White Christians did not remember the blood-stained cross as a symbol of solidarity. In fact, back then, that cross would have been lit on fire and placed and co-opted by a hate group called the Ku Klux Klan. They did not remember the nails that penetrated through the hands and feet of Jesus into that cross, sealing his efforts. Instead, they compounded the sin with the collusion of the full network available: the medical examiner, the police department, and civilian witnesses. It was the modern-day network analogous to Pharisees, Roman soldiers, Pontius Pilate, and the angry mob of Jews that collaborated to wrongfully and tragically execute a poor Brown-skinned man from the margins who posed a threat to them by his very existence.

My grandfather's legacy is lived out through the grandchildren he never knew. His spirit of resistance and fight has new life today. His blood cries out from the earth and from my life; our lives are megaphones that amplify it, calling my white and non-Black brothers and sisters to a multigenerational show of solidarity against anti-Black racism. This is not to say that racism does not impact other groups and that Black people need not concern themselves with their respective plights. This is to acknowledge that as the African American community is lifted up from the bottom of the racialized boot of white supremacy that has left 401 years of footprints on our backs, everyone else is lifted up as well. As white supremacy is forced to remove the knee that replaced the chains and the nooses around our necks, taking our lives, it benefits all. The protests today are not just for George Floyd but for the lineage of Black bodies left to die at the hands of white men or at the word of white women. The protests today are for the African bodies that never made it across the Atlantic Ocean. They are walking for the enslaved Africans who did not survive 246 years of slavery. They are chanting for the 6,500-plus Black bodies hung from trees across the United States postslavery. They are raising fists in the air for the countless Black bodies with no names, unmarked graves, and unsolved murders. They are angry today for those Black lives taken, including my grandfather, Nate Allen. The world is remembering him too.

Martin Luther King Jr. once called the voices of resistance to a new movement for justice "the death groans from a dying system."[7] Unfortunately, the church is guilty of making these death groans. He goes on to say, "But history has proven that social systems have a great last-minute breathing power."[8] The white evangelical church and the conservative corners of US society are competing with the African American community for air. This old system of thought and its ethos is attempting to suck the air out of our bodies. We can't breathe. We are still suffocating under the oppressive social structures that many fight to sustain. They have erected scaffolding alongside these old systems, attempting to present them fresh in new ways. They erase or reframe history and theology and convince a portion of the country to join a movement to "Make America Great Again." Meanwhile, we can't breathe.

But I must breathe. I must take the breaths that my grandfather could not. I must take the breaths that were taken away from him with a single bullet. I must breathe as I bear my cross saying, "It is *not* finished." The work of racial justice, equality, and equity is not finished. Honoring my grandfather and the millions of Black lives lost at the hands of white supremacy is not finished. What was finished through Jesus at the cross was the power of evil and sin to overcome these righteous efforts. Maybe the next generation of Allens and Black activists and non-Black allies will say, "We *can* breathe!"

Reflection Questions

Which term do you prefer to use and work toward: *racial reconciliation* or *racial solidarity*? Why?

How have you positioned yourself in solidaric work that reflects the solidarity witnessed in Jesus's willingness to die on the cross for humanity?

Afterword

Where Do We Go from Here?

Oftentimes people ask the question, What do we do next? Usually they are eager to initiate or join a movement to confront racism. The tendency is to find steps to engage or fix the problem. For white people, this should not be what they consider first. Rather than seeking what to do, they ought to pursue who they ought to become by subjecting themselves to the "soul work" necessary to advocate for true deep cultural change as it relates to racism. There has to be work that God does on the inside of their hearts and minds through the "dance" they have done with communities of color and with God. There has to be transformation or else they will bring their privilege and power and function in them as they have been socialized to and ultimately produce little in the form of cultural transformation. The new course of maturity should then impart humility, wisdom, and discernment as to what "ought" to be done.

Let me recap the event in one of my classes in seminary that was integral in forming my thoughts on what we can do next. When I shared my grandfather's story for the first time, I was surprised by the response of my white classmates.

After watching a clip of the documentary series *Eyes on the Prize* narrating the story of the murder of Emmett Till, the seeds of what ought to happen next to progress significantly toward racial justice were planted. The class was asked to break up into small groups and discuss the video. The revelation came in the response of my classmates after hearing my comments regarding Till reminding me of my grandfather because of the similarities of their murders. Till's body was found after being shot and thrown in the Tallahatchie River. He was unrecognizable. The men who killed him, though tried, were found not guilty for the murder. The family never received justice for Emmett Till's death.

When we broke into small groups, my group included two white classmates, one male and one female. I began to share for the first time outside of close friends the story of my grandfather's murder. My first words were, "I can't look at the pictures of Emmett Till without seeing my grandfather." There was silence. I even needed a moment to process what I had just shared. What happened as I continued to summarize the story for them pleasantly surprised me. I began to see tears in both of their eyes as they listened. I was surprised because I had never experienced any white person visibly react so deeply with empathy about the racial tragedies that had plagued African Americans, especially regarding my family's story. While I've never really shared my family's story before, I had shared the story of Till, Medgar Evers, and other African Americans who had been murdered "at the hands of white supremacy."

What unfolded during that short conversation with classmates was the journey that I believe white people must take in order to be a part of the solution. What I learned is that in this work, there is no place for neutrality. Neutrality is an ally for injustice because neutrality tolerates unjust attitudes, words, and actions like those that would be considered racist. A neutral stance on racism is a safe space for it to thrive. Their actions in just a few moments provided a blueprint for what needs to be done next. They *listened*, *learned*, and *lamented* and were ready to *labor* for the cause of racial justice. During class, I wrote down those four words and believed that they were significant steps for moving forward.

Listen

So what does it look like to execute these sequential alliterated steps? To be clear, this is unapologetically directed toward white people. People of color, for the most part, but with exceptions, desire to cause or at least see social change. There are many white people who are allies in the sense that they too desire to actively participate in the work for social/racial justice. This is for the large majority of white people who are racists, nonracist but indifferent and silent, or zealous but still operate from privilege with the residue of the ideology of white supremacy.

First, white people must be willing to *listen* like my classmates. White people should be willing to enter into spaces of color where conversations around racism are engaged with the desire to hear them. They should listen to the stories and testimonies of people of color as they share their legitimate experiences and perspectives. They should be willing to sit in the discomfort of voices that cause them to have to think critically about their own whiteness. Even if they are listening to the stories, the history, and the experiences of people of color in the comfort of their own homes, nevertheless, they are still immersing themselves, to a degree, in the culture.

Listening to stories from African Americans and other people of color can educate white people on whiteness as much as it can on Blackness or otherness. Listening well forces a person to have to be mindful of the presuppositions and preconceived ideas they bring to the conversation. It makes the person take a self-assessment of the mental and social paradigms they operate from that inform their understanding of self, others, and how God may be active within creation. For example, to hear my family's story takes a dark part of American history that seems so far away and irrelevant and brings it to the forefront of their minds and forces them to have to wrestle with the implications of that history on us today.

The practice of listening is inherently reverential. A white person willing to listen says to people of color that their stories more than matter, but they are sacred. When you enter the space of the sacred, you enter with humility to be present rather than to dictate the terms of occupying that space. I agree with Soong-Chan Rah when he writes in *Prophetic Lament*, "The tendency to view the holistic work of the church as the action of the privileged *toward* the marginalized often derails the work of true community healing."[1] This undermines a fundamental characteristic of the work of solidarity. Solidarity, by nature, requires a joining of selves, not the imposition of one's self—mind, body, and spirit—especially of those in power entering the space of the marginalized "other." Listening offers space for this wisdom and discernment. It may be a catalyst for more questions, which leads to learning, which deepens the solidaric relationship that has been fostered.

There is another kind of listening that is often overlooked. White people must listen to their own bodies. They must be willing to be honest about and articulate how they are feeling when they sit in the discomfort of the stories being told. They ought to be attentive to their own biomarkers. In listening, they can then ask questions. They can ask themselves, "Am I angry?" "Why do I feel a sense of anxiety?" "Where is my anger directed?" "Am I angry at the history or the current systems and structures, or am I angry at African Americans for disrupting my comfort?" This listening will go a long way in understanding any underlying issues that need to be addressed before or while moving forward to engage in the work of racial justice. White people must be aware of what may be triggering or retraumatizing them because this work requires them to be healthy.

Learn

Listening is a foundational skill for *learning*. Storytelling by people of color has a pedagogical function, but what white people may need to learn is much more than the informality of storytelling. White people should position themselves to learn from professors, preachers, theologians, philosophers, and authors of color. All my life, from the time I can remember, almost all of the textbooks I read were written and edited by white people. This means a Eurocentric perspective has largely shaped my education. If this is true for me, then it is absolutely true for the vast majority of white people, with the exception of those who chose to learn from scholars of color. This white perspective on history, theology, and culture is not only the dominant view but, like whiteness in general, the standard by which all other perspectives are measured.

What is at stake is an epistemology that is fractured and deformed by whiteness. American history told from a white perspective often leaves out the depth of pain brought on by events and eras that severely oppressed people of color. Respected historical figures are presented in their best light, where their involvement in events like the enslavement of Africans, the massacre and forced assimilation of Native people, and Japanese concentration camps are footnotes in historical accounts. American church history as told from a white perspective often conveniently leaves out the church's complicity with racism, but it also leaves out theology from the margins. I am certain that the theology of the slave owners was not in agreement with the theology of the enslaved Africans who would become Christians. The contributions of people of color to the progress and prosperity of the United States are often minimized in deference to the contributions of white Americans. If whiteness is the source of one's epistemology, that knowledge is deficient in its truth and facts.

Learning from people of color gives white people an opportunity to grow beyond their whiteness. As Willie Jennings claims, whiteness deforms one's maturity; ironically, it is white people whose maturity is arguably the most deformed. The world as we know it has been reoriented around whiteness. For white Christians, even God is oriented around whiteness. The easiest example is presenting the historical Jesus, the God-man, in a European body. Whiteness has socialized white people—and some people of color—to see themselves in everything to the point where whiteness is natural and normal and erases the "otherized" people of color. This is true for what is materially white—white skin and other physical features—and what is white in the abstract, like theology, the biblical narrative, philosophy, and so on. But this is only one perspective in the world. To marginalize all others in ways that prevent learning from them stunts the growth of all, especially white people.

Learning particularly from African Americans generates a necessary level of respect for Blackness that whiteness on its own cannot provide. I was engaged in a debate on an online platform with an Asian American student who was vocal about his displeasure in the Black student concerns around race issues at the seminary I attend. In his defense of white professors, he claims (and I paraphrase) that the school hires the best professors, so why should they compromise on the quality of scholars just to meet a quota by hiring Black professors. What he may or may not have realized in this statement is that he is saying the best professors are white professors and hiring Black professors would be lowering the standard in quality of teaching. Sadly, this is not foreign to the thinking of many people of all races.

I realized in my undergrad studies at a Bible college in the Los Angeles area that almost all of my professors besides one were white. Just about all of the authors and theologians in the reading lists were white. There was at least one author in one of my reading lists who was a well-known pastor before and during the time of the civil rights movement who was a known segregationist and justified his position theologically. I was expected to learn from him. I was expected to accept being shaped by white theology at that school. It is important to learn from people of color because this is the only way of breaking up the hegemony of whiteness in shaping the minds of generations to follow.

Learning invites a revised worldview and an updated trajectory of one's life and calling. I often teach in my spheres of influence that as we grow in our understanding of who God is, we must be willing to *unlearn* what we have been taught about God. In their learning, white people must unlearn what they have understood about Black people, about the United States, and even about themselves. It is only after this deconstruction that they will be able to make room for and reconstruct a new paradigm for race and capture the vision of a new deracialized (or less-racialized) America.

Lament

Listening and learning should lead to *lament*. Lament is the response of grief and sorrow to suffering and pain. It is a liturgical response,[2] as Rah writes, but it also ought to be communal and personal. My classmates displayed lament when their tears filled their eyes and raced down their faces. I felt the sincerity of their grief for my family's pain from the trauma of losing my grandfather to the wickedness of racism. I had never personally seen or felt lament from a white person over issues of racial injustice before. This exceeded the intellectual response that merely acknowledges how bad racist incidents like this are. It always seemed as if the heady responses still allowed white people to detach themselves from the incident or the kind of person who would do or say such a thing. The young man in my small group shared that after hearing my story, as I was seeing my grandfather in Emmett Till, he was seeing *his* grandfather in the men who killed Till and in the man who killed my grandfather. His grief did not allow him to detach himself from the event. Instead, he drew nearer to it by placing his own flesh and blood in the faces and bodies of the men who embodied the same white supremacist ideology that his grandfather would have.

Lament is the catalyst to action. Rarely do we as human beings engage in anything beyond our comfort without a burden from the depths of our being. Theologically speaking, this is the work of the Holy Spirit compelling us to action with the weightiness of conviction. When the community laments together, they participate with God in response to an individual or a group's suffering. Those who suffer are seen and are affirmed by the community and/or individuals that they matter and the fact that they are suffering matters.

There is healing potential in shared lament. As I watched Till's body and visualized my own grandfather, I could feel it in my body. I could feel a nervous energy, elevated blood pressure, and grief. My body began to relax as I shared my thoughts, but when I saw the tears of my classmates, there was an overwhelming sense of peace that overcame me. Suddenly, grief gave way to make space for joy and a sense of the beginning of healing. More importantly, I felt safe in that space. I had more confidence in those tears than I ever could in an apology or eloquent speech. I trusted the wordlessness of those tears to convey the authenticity of their solidarity. Those tears conveyed the potential for collaborative work with my white classmates.

Labor

The fruit of all the inner work of listening, learning, and lamenting is *labor*. This is where "doing" begins. To invest in the work of disrupting social structures that have historically produced inequities and injustices in American society without doing the "soul work" would be counterproductive. Without the "soul work," well-meaning white brothers and sisters will still operate from the same privilege and power standpoint that produced the racialized structures in the first place. Whiteness has to be deconstructed and white people given new eyes, new thinking, new feelings in their bodies than before. This is imperative for two reasons; although this list is not exhaustive, it is important to note. White people do not feel the brunt of racism—although they may see its fruit in communities of color if they were to pay attention. Without feeling this in their bodies, they will not have the same sense of urgency or even desperation that communities of color do. They won't operate with the same degree of passion. It may simply be another quick fix compassion project that lasts temporarily but makes no substantial change.

The other reason labor must follow "soul work" is because of the natural inclination for whiteness or power to preserve itself. In other words, there is only so far they will be able—or in some cases, willing—to go to transform society. If we think theologically, we may want to consider what Jesus asked of the rich young ruler in Mark 10. When approaching Jesus to ask about what he needed to do to obtain eternal life, Jesus pointed him to the commandments. He insisted that he had done all those things. Although this pleased Jesus, Jesus told him he lacked one thing; he needed to essentially give up everything he owned in order to follow Jesus. I share this not to emphasize the "following Jesus" part—though this is of utmost importance. I am emphasizing the more universal aspect of what Jesus said. As it relates to the work of racial justice and solidarity, white people, to follow or walk alongside African Americans and people color in this journey, need to be willing to give up everything. They will need to consider the relationships, ideologies, privilege, security, and so on that may hinder their ability to do what is necessary to achieve justice and solidarity.

White Christians should consider that life is at stake for many people of color. A recent example is seen in how

COVID-19, a highly contagious virus that knows no boundaries and is no respecter of person, kills Black and Brown people at a higher rate largely because of the legacy of racialized structures that have left communities of color more vulnerable than white communities in general. This is life or death, especially for African Americans. Whiteness, or white supremacy, has destroyed us from the slave trade to slavery, to Jim Crow, to mass incarceration, to police shootings, and to pandemics. This is why white people should not take the lead in this cause, but their collaborative participation and presence is necessary for progress. Without the embodied experience of being Black and on the receiving end of racism, they will only be able to go so far in terms of solutions. It requires mind, body, and spirit invested in this fight.

The labor is deeply spiritual. At its roots is a network of what the apostle Paul would describe as powers and principalities, rulers, and cosmic forces that manifest themselves in the material world.[3] This is not to hyperspiritualize the issue and absolve human agency that aligns with these spiritual entities, but it is to recognize the root of the issue. This requires the work of exorcism. I use exorcism not in a literal sense but in a figurative sense, although a religious argument may be made for both. These cosmic roots show up in persons (dominions/lord), institutions (authorities), and systems (principalities), according to Max Stackhouse.[4] In other words, these manifestations of racism have spiritual roots, and the spiritual entities have human and structural agencies. If Paul is correct, the labor must begin with prayer. Otherwise, we place futile hopes on humanistic efforts to eradicate spiritual forces and the material to combat the spiritual.

Even Martin Luther King Jr. grounded his direct action efforts on a spiritual foundation. King writes, "This method is passive physically but strongly active spiritually; it is non-aggressive physically but dynamically aggressive spiritually."[5] He drew from the life and practices of Jesus and Gandhi. King grounded his nonviolent direct action in the Christian ethic of love, which he calls "the most durable power in the world."[6] In "Letter from Birmingham City Jail," King outlines the four basic steps for his direct action campaign: (1) collection of the facts, (2) negotiation, (3) *self-purification*, and (4) direct action.[7] Before the execution of direct action in the form of marches, sit-ins, and rallies, there needed to be an emptying of oneself in order to endure the battle that ensued. It is also this self-emptying that makes space for the love of God and the love of those who you sacrifice for and stand with in solidarity for the cause of righting wrongs. The same is the case in the cause today. This is a centuries-old evil that has endured revivals and social unrest by morphing in some ways and resurrecting more recognizable ones.

Ahmaud Arbery, Eric Garner, Tamir Rice, and George Floyd's murders—just to name a few—bring back memories of the past where Black men found themselves at the mercy of white violence in the streets. Breonna Taylor and Atatiana Jefferson's murders remind us of the limitlessness of white supremacy to invade homes to take Black life. White supremacy has evolved and morphed in secrecy, and it has remained predictably the same while being emboldened to afflict trauma.

Nate Allen is one of thousands of Black bodies left lifeless at the hands of a white supremacy that is not held accountable to the degree in which it must. However, the labor must continue. It is spiritual and practical. It is collaborative and requires all hands on deck. The labor will not be in vain because the next generations, though they will have to continue the fight, will have different conversations and will hopefully be closer to postracial than our generation will ever witness. My story has been one long nightmare for my family. It has been felt and carried in our bodies, in many cases without us even realizing it. But the dream is in the audacity to confront such injustices in order to right the wrongs and participate in redemption. This labor is the work of healing the *open wounds*.

Reflection Questions

Have you identified the soul work that needs to be done in you to participate in the work of social/racial justice? If so, are you willing to do the inner work?

Which of these four factors—listen, learn, lament, and labor—resonates with you the most? Which do you think you need to improve upon? Which appears to be the most challenging?

Notes

Chapter 1

1 Roy Bryant and J. W. Milam admitted in a January 24, 1956, interview with *Look* magazine that they had beaten and shot Till and threw his body in the Tallahatchie River. They were paid $4,000 for the interview.

2 "Always in Season," Always in Season Film, accessed June 10, 2020, https://www.alwaysinseasonfilm.com/. This story was captured in the 2019 documentary *Always in Season*. The story details the evidence found and the details surrounding the young man's death such as details of the scene, altercations days before his murder with a known racist couple, his involvement with an older white woman who lived with the racist couple, the couple's sudden relocation away from Bladensboro soon after Lacy's death. The family is left to try and heal from the trauma.

3 *Usual Suspects*, directed by Bryan Singer (Universal City, CA: Gramercy Pictures, 1995).

4 Martin Luther King Jr., *Strength to Love* (Minneapolis, MN: Fortress Press, 2010), 25.

Chapter 2

1 Maya Angelou is widely credited with this quote. The source for this quote (book, poem, interview, etc.) is unknown to the author.

2 Steve Williams, "Do Not Go Gentle into That Good Night," *South Strand News*, September 5, 2018, https://tinyurl.com/y6conhwu.

3 Williams.

4 Bryan Stevenson, "Lynching in America: Targeting Black Veterans," Equal Justice Initiative, accessed July 9, 2019, https://tinyurl.com/y4a5wqcs.

Chapter 4

1 *Online Etymology Dictionary*, s.v. "trauma," accessed April 14, 2020, https://tinyurl.com/y3xvyzk7.

2 *Online Etymology Dictionary*, s.v. "tere," accessed April 14, 2020, https://tinyurl.com/y4nxut9h.

3 Shelley Rambo, *Spirit and Trauma: A Theology of Remaining* (Louisville, KY: Westminster John Knox Press, 2010), 4, 7 (emphasis mine), Kindle.

4 *CTE* is a term "used to describe brain degeneration likely caused by repeated head trauma." Mayo Clinic Staff, "Chronic Traumatic Encephalopathy," June 4, 2019, https://tinyurl.com/y4u2t5fs.

5 Andrew Sung Park, *Racial Conflict and Healing: An Asian-American Theological Perspective* (Eugene, OR: Wipf and Stock, 2009), 9.

6 Resmaa Menakem, *My Grandmother's Hands: Racialized Trauma and the Pathway to Mending Our Hearts and Bodies* (Las Vegas, NV: Central Recovery, 2017), 89, Kindle.

7 Bessel Van Der Kolk, *The Body Keeps the Score: Brain, Mind, and Body in the Healing of Trauma* (New York: Penguin, 2014).

8 A study released in 2020 by Equal Justice Initiative (EJI) reported that nearly two thousand African Americans were lynched during the twelve years of Reconstruction. Equal Justice Initiative, "Reconstruction in America: Racial Violence after the Civil War, 1865–1876," 2020, https://tinyurl.com/y5s6rzza.

9 James H. Cone, *God of the Oppressed* (Maryknoll, NY: Orbis, 1997).

Chapter 5

1 Vincent Lloyd, introduction to *Race and Secularism in America*, ed. Jonathon S. Kahn and Vincent W. Lloyd (New York: Columbia University Press, 2016), 4, Kindle.

Chapter 6

1 Matt Vautour, "Black Lives Matter: NFL Pledges $250 Million to 'Combat Systemic Racism,'" MSN, June 11, 2020, https://tinyurl.com/y2lupyv2.
2 Apple Dictionary, s.v. "Rhythm," accessed April 20, 2020.
3 Kim Severson, "Number of US Hate Groups Is Rising, Report Says," *New York Times*, March 7, 2012, https://tinyurl.com/yykfsk6m.
4 Willie J. Jennings, "Can 'White' People Be Saved?," in *Can "White" People Be Saved? Triangulating Race, Theology, and Missions*, ed. Love L. Sechrest, Johnny Ramirez-Johnson, and Amos Yong (Downers Grove, IL: IVP Academic, 2018), 29.
5 Love Sechrest and Johnny Ramirez-Johnson, eds., introduction to *Can "White" People Be Saved?*, 12 (emphasis mine). See Jennings, "Can 'White' People Be Saved?"

Chapter 7

1 Resmaa Menakem, *My Grandmother's Hands: Racialized Trauma and the Pathway to Mending Our Hearts and Bodies* (Las Vegas, NV: Central Recovery, 2017), 101 (emphasis mine), Kindle.

2 Menakem, 102.

3 Robin DiAngelo, *White Fragility: Why It's So Hard for White People to Talk about Racism* (Boston, MA: Beacon, 2018), 1, Kindle.

4 Menakem, *My Grandmother's Hands*, 99–100.

Chapter 8

1 *Online Etymology Dictionary*, s.v. "wise," accessed April 15, 2020, https://tinyurl.com/yat69af8.

2 *Online Etymology Dictionary*, s.v. "-dom," accessed April 15, 2020, https://tinyurl.com/yym87c8m.

Chapter 9

1 Samuel R. Gross, ed., "Race and Wrongful Convictions in the United States," National Registry of Exonerations, March 7, 2017, https://tinyurl.com/gp5d866.

2 Isaiah 7:14 and Matthew 1:23.

3 Philippians 2:7–8.

4 Phil Allen Jr., "Power-Full Black Bodily Resistance: Reimagining Kaepernick's Protest through King's Nonviolent Direct Action," *Journal of Religious Leadership* 18, no. 2 (Autumn 2019): 39.

5 Luke 4:18.

6 Luke 22:42.

7 Martin Luther King Jr., "Facing the Challenge of a New Age," in *A Testament of Hope: Essential Writings and Speeches of Martin Luther King, Jr.*, ed. James M. Washington (New York: Harper One, 1986), 138.

8 King Jr., 141.

Afterword

1 Soong-Chan Rah, *Prophetic Lament: A Call for Justice in Troubled Times* (Downers Grove, IL: IVP, 2015), 21 (emphasis mine), Kindle.

2 Rah, 21.

3 Ephesians 6:12 (ESV): "We do not wrestle against flesh and blood, but against the rulers, against the authorities, against the cosmic powers over this present darkness, against the spiritual forces of evil in the heavenly places."

4 Max L. Stackhouse, "General Introduction," in *God and Globalization*, vol. 1, *Religion and Powers of the Common Life*, ed. Max L. Stackhouse and Peter J. Paris (New York: Trinity International, 2000), 31–52.

5 Martin Luther King Jr., "Nonviolence and Racial Justice," in *A Testament of Hope: Essential Writings and Speeches of Martin Luther King, Jr.*, ed. James M. Washington (New York: Harper One, 1986), 7.

6 Martin Luther King Jr., "The Most Durable Power," in *Testament of Hope*, 11.

7 Martin Luther King Jr., "Letter from Birmingham City Jail," in *Testament of Hope*, 290.